W9-BZX-101

An Insider's Guide to Refinancing Your Mortgage

An Insider's Guide to Refinancing Your Mortgage

Money-Saving Secrets You Need to Know

DAVID REED

ᴬMACOM

American Management Association

New York • Atlanta • Brussels • Chicago • Mexico City • San Francisco
Shanghai • Tokyo • Toronto • Washington, D.C.

Special discounts on bulk quantities of AMACOM books are available to corporations, professional associations, and other organizations. For details, contact Special Sales Department, AMACOM, a division of American Management Association, 1601 Broadway, New York, NY 10019.
Tel: 212-903-8316. Fax: 212-903-8083.
E-mail: specialsls@amanet.org
Website: www.amacombooks.org/go/specialsales
To view all AMACOM titles go to: www.amacombooks.org

This publication is designed to provide accurate and authoritative information in regard to the subject matter covered. It is sold with the understanding that the publisher is not engaged in rendering legal, accounting, or other professional service. If legal advice or other expert assistance is required, the services of a competent professional person should be sought.

REALTOR® is a Registered collective membership mark that identifies a real estate professional who is a member of the National Association of REALTORS® and subscribes to its strict Code of Ethics. AMACOM uses these names throughout this book in initial capital letters or ALL CAPITAL letters for editorial purposes only, with no intention of trademark violation.

Library of Congress Cataloging-in-Publication Data

Reed, David (Carl David), 1957–
   An insider's guide to refinancing your mortgage : money-saving secrets you need to know / David Reed.
      p.   cm.
   ISBN 978-0-8144-0935-0
   1. Mortgage loans—United States—Refinancing.   I. Title

HG2040.5.U5R428   2009
332.7′22—dc22

                              2008020999

© 2009 by David Reed
All rights reserved.
Printed in the United States of America.

This publication may not be reproduced, stored in a retrieval system, or transmitted in whole or in part, in any form or by any means, electronic, mechanical, photocopying, recording, or otherwise, without the prior written permission of AMACOM, a division of American Management Association, 1601 Broadway, New York, NY 10019.

Printing number

10 9 8 7 6 5 4 3 2 1

This book is dedicated to Brenda, Philip, Tena, Wendy, and Paul

Contents

Introduction

Having been in the mortgage business for nearly two decades, I've seen mortgage companies come and go. And I've seen mortgage loan programs come and go along with them.

Technology has made an impact on the mortgage industry. Mortgage loan approvals used to take several weeks to accomplish. Now, it's only a matter of days. Loans are approved using automated systems and no longer need human beings making judgment calls as to the borrower's creditworthiness.

Since loans are so easy to approve and take very little time to complete, the entry-level qualifications for loan officers are very low. Sure, loan officers have to get licensed in the state where they place mortgage loans. But trust me, the licensing procedure is typically nothing more than taking a rudimentary test and getting fingerprinted. There are more inexperienced loan officers in this business than ever before, all trying to get a piece of the "refinance pie."

Because of the ease of mortgage approvals, interest rates don't have to fall very much in order to make a refinance a reasonable proposition. And mortgage companies, in all their glory, can market themselves silly trying to convince you to refinance your loan with them. Heck, there are even classes that loan officers can take to learn how to convince you to refinance your mortgage.

Kids going to college? There's a refinance plan. Need retirement funds? There's a plan. Need to reduce your monthly payments? There's a plan for that, too.

The problem with all that is those "plans" are nothing more than variations on the very same loan program. The only difference: a new sales script has been written to fit the advertisement. And don't get me wrong, these "scripts" can be convincing. Loan officers don't get paid until they close a loan, so you can't blame them for trying to stoke their livelihood. But don't get too excited about those solicitations until you read this book.

Having been in the business so long, I've closed more mortgage loans than most loan officers have. I have also observed how the markets have developed over the years, how loan programs have evolved, and how technology has impacted the mortgage industry.

The mortgage business can be intimidating. Its jargon can be confusing, at best, and deceitful, at worst. Lenders make loans all day long, while you may only get a mortgage a few times in your life.

Refinancing your mortgage takes more planning than when you were searching for a loan to *buy* your home. When you bought your property, you were focused on the "big picture." You needed to close on time, the property needed to pass inspection, there were property taxes to be paid, and so on. But with a refinance, you're focused on one thing and one thing only: your loan.

◆ CHAPTER ONE ◆

What Is a Refinance?

> **re·fi′nance** *n.* To provide new financing to replace previous financing, using different terms, rates, or loan amounts.

There. Pretty simple, is it not? If refinancing your mortgage were that easy, this would be a very short book. After all, in order to refinance you must have had a previous mortgage, meaning that you've already been through all this. But refinancing can be a tricky business. A refinance costs money, and if you choose the wrong term or rate, your mistakes can cost thousands upon thousands of dollars in lost interest and needless closing costs.

There are loan officers who do nothing but refinances. They take classes that show them how to contact their old customers and talk them into a refinance mortgage. Pull cash out! Pay for college! Fix up that home! Lower your rate! Lower your payment! It's trickier than that, though. When you bought the property in the first place, your goal was to find a competitive rate at a reasonable cost for a mortgage. But refinancing takes much more analysis than picking up the phone and getting a rate quote.

There are more reasons to refinance than you can imagine. And there are times when it's not good to refinance, no matter what the loan officer told you over the phone. I'm sure you've heard the advertisements on the radio proclaiming, "Lower your payments by half!" or "$400,000 mortgage for only $350 per month!" Ever wonder how lenders can make such claims? Well, partly because they're true. There really *are* loans that can dramatically lower your monthly payments. But did that lender also tell you that if you did make that low a payment, your loan balance will actually get *larger* instead of being paid down?

Lenders can attempt to make any refinance loan more attractive than it really is. They don't make money unless they are making loans, so they try to invent new mortgage programs that might be enticing to you. Or they can be predatory in nature, refinancing your mortgage over and over again, stripping out any equity you may have in the property or putting you into a mortgage loan with some very bad terms in it. It's bad enough that people lose their homes.

Refinancing is an opportunity to sweeten the terms of your current note or to take advantage of new, lower rates and save on mortgage interest—but only if you do it the right away and avoid the traps unsuspecting consumers fall into.

Refinancing Your Home Loan

Refinance loans adhere to the same credit standards as purchase money loans. A *purchase money loan* is a loan used to buy and finance real estate. It would seem to make sense that if you're lowering your monthly payment, then a lender would automatically approve your loan, since you've been making the higher payments on time. But your loan will be evaluated and, perhaps, approved in the very same fashion as when you purchased the property by means of credit, income, and assets. You will make a loan application on the very same form that you used when you purchased the property, and the lender will typically ask for the same old stuff, such as pay stubs and bank statements.

There are times when people go through a bad patch after they've purchased a home. Perhaps they've lost a job or there was an illness in the family, and they fell behind on their mortgage or other credit payments. When credit becomes a concern, it's quite possible that, regardless of how much lower a payment will be after a refinance, it won't be approved for a refinance loan if it doesn't fit the credit standards of conventional lending.

One caveat here. Government-backed loans such as *VA loans*—which are government mortgages guaranteed by the Department of Veteran Affairs—and *FHA loans*—which are insured by the Federal Housing Administration—do have an advantage over all other refinance types. It's called a *streamline refinance*, and as long as the monthly payment is being reduced, then credit or income is hardly an issue. You have to currently have an FHA or VA loan to qualify for the streamline. You cannot simply refinance into one. A streamline refinance asks for less documentation and has few if any credit guidelines, other than not being late on the mortgage payment for the previous 12 months.

Loans are approved a bit differently from the way they were a few years ago. Every lender now uses a system called an *Automated Underwriting System, or AUS,* to approve their loans, instead of sending the loan to an underwriter who will manually determine if the loan file meets lending guidelines.

An AUS reviews the borrower's loan application in its entirety, along with the credit report and the loan amount compared to the appraised value—all in about 15 seconds. With an AUS approval, other factors are taken into consideration that might override a negative item in a credit report, which is how lenders advertise "Instant Approvals" on their websites or in other promotional pieces. For instance, if there are some late payments or even collection accounts in a person's credit file, but if there were also other mitigating factors, such as good income or a hefty equity position, then sometimes an approval can be had with the best rates, as long as the AUS comes back "Approved." Still, credit that has been damaged since the original purchase must have significant offsetting positives in the file for an AUS to issue an approval.

There are other positives when using an AUS, and one of those is how the file will be documented. A *strong file* will require little documentation; a *weak file* will require more documentation.

An example of a strong file would be an applicant with:

Low loan amount, compared to the value
Loan amount = $200,000
Property value = $500,000

◆ ◆ ◆

Low debt-to-income ratios
Income = $5,000 per month
Debt = $1,000 per month
Excellent credit with no late payments and high credit scores

An example of a weak file would be an applicant with:

High loan amount, compared to value
Loan amount = $200,000
Property value = $210,000

♦ ♦ ♦

High debt-to-income ratios
Income = $5,000 per month
Debt = $2,500 per month
Decent credit with a few late payments and moderate credit scores

The weaker the file, the more documentation will be required to complete the loan. For instance, a weak file may require:

- Two most recent pay stubs

- W2s from the previous year

- Three months' worth of bank and investment statements

- A full appraisal

A strong file would require:

- A *verbal verification* of employment by the lender, which simply means calling up the applicant's employer and making sure she works there. That's it.

Because of the AUS, it's not really necessary to start digging up old tax returns, bank statements, or investment account statements before you even apply for a mortgage. Instead, just turn in the loan application and wait for the approval. The approval will list exactly the items needed to close your loan—no more, no less.

Regardless of the amount of documentation the AUS asks for, sometimes there are other documentation levels for a refinance that are requested of the borrower instead of being asked of by the AUS. Documentation, which includes everything associated with income and assets, can vary depending upon the loan type. There are several different types of loan documentation levels for a refinance, independent of any AUS decision. Those levels are called:

- Full documentation

- Stated documentation

- No documentation

A *fully documented loan* is one where everything is verified using third-party verification methods. *Third party* means that it has to be verified by someone not related to the borrower. For income purposes, that would mean providing pay check stubs or last year's W2. To verify assets, the lender might complete a *Verification of Deposit* form, or VOD, and mail it to the borrower's bank, or the borrower might supply the most recent statements from a bank or investment account. Most loans are fully documented.

A *stated documentation loan* is one in which whatever the borrower puts on the loan application, that's what the lender uses to approve the loan. If the borrower claims he or she makes $5,000 per month, then that's what the lender will use when calculating debt-to-income ratios. Or perhaps the borrower puts down that he has $100,000 in his checking account; the lender will use that $100,000 number without verifying the amount.

Finally, a *no documentation loan,* or *no doc,* is one where no income, employment, or asset information is put on the application whatsoever. Nothing—no job, no income, and no bank accounts.

Do borrowers really have a choice as to the level of documentation they wish to provide to the lender? Lenders do offer such programs, but of course there's a catch: you might qualify for a no documentation loan, but that loan might require higher credit scores, a 20 percent down payment, and a stipulation that you must occupy the property and not use a no doc loan for investment purposes. Interest rates are higher for no doc loans, as well. Stated documentation loans also are available from many lenders, but again, they require more down payment and ask for a higher interest rate than a fully documented loan.

Lenders can be flexible with borrowers, but only when it makes sense to them. By introducing a new element of risk when evaluating a home loan request, such as not documenting a borrower's income or employment, the lender will offset that risk with higher rates and fees. Such alternative documentation methods are available because sometimes income does indeed exist, but that income does not meet the lender's income criteria.

A common income requirement might be that a self-employed person must prove he or she has been so employed for two years, before any income can be used. The lender will average the borrower's income from the previous two years. Averaging income sometimes doesn't tell *all* the story, though. If a borrower wasn't self-employed for two years (as with an attorney fresh out of school or a restaurant owner who had a terrible year two years ago, but a great year last year) that would mean his average income might not qualify him for a fully documented loan. It's not that the income isn't there; it is, but it doesn't fit the lender's guidelines for income.

Someone with a strong credit profile may also see an extra benefit, receiving an *appraisal waiver*, which is one in which you don't have to have an appraisal performed, thus saving you about $350 or more. This doesn't mean the AUS doesn't care about the value; it certainly does. But the AUS has a component of its approval method called an *Automated Valuation Model*, or *AVM*, which will research the local database of public records and scour recent sales in your zip code, indicating a reasonable valuation of your home. If you want to refinance $200,000, and you think your property would appraise at $300,000, then you would simply enter the $300,000 value on the application and wait to see if you were granted an appraisal waiver.

An appraisal waiver can be critical if you think you may run into valuation problems, such as having a high loan amount compared to your value. Typically, any loan amount that exceeds 80 percent of the value of the home will require a *private mortgage insurance policy*, or *PMI*. PMI is an insurance policy that pays a lender a predetermined amount, should a borrower who puts less than 20 percent default on the note. If you think you may have some valuation issues, or you simply aren't sure what the values are, then it's better to "guess" on the high side rather than the low side. If you have a strong credit profile, it's possible you'll get the appraisal waiver and the AUS will simply use whatever value you put on your application.

Valuation is a key component when refinancing. Refinances can't go above 95 percent of the value of the property, in most cases, and can't be done at all if the property is "upside down," meaning that the property is worth less than the amounts owed on it. There are times when property values in a local area decline, usually due to a downturn in the economy. People lose their jobs or move where there are better jobs, and suddenly there are more homes on the market than there are buyers. Home prices begin to shrink; they can shrink so much that their value is less than what is owed on the property. Regardless of how much lower rates are, or how much lower one could get his monthly payment, a lender absolutely will not refinance a loan when the loan amount is greater than 100 percent of the value. And that limitation is for primary residences. Investment properties have a stricter valuation guideline and won't allow for a refinance if the loan amount exceeds 90 percent of the value of the home. Appraisal waivers are also rare for investment properties.

Appraised value also must be "seasoned," which occurs one year after the original purchase. No matter what kind of deal you got on your new purchase, lenders will wait until one year after the sale date to determine value for a refinance. Let's say you got an unheard of deal on a house in a nice neighborhood. You paid $300,000 for a $500,000 home. Lenders will make the initial mortgage based upon the lower of the sales price or appraised value. In this instance, the lender would base the loan on a sales price of $300,000, even if the appraised value came in at $350,000. This approach accomplishes two things for the lender: (1) the buyer must still put some money into the transaction, and (2) it allows for time to truly establish a market value.

When a buyer looks at a home, sees an appraised value of $350,000, and gets a contract on it for $300,000, that buyer doesn't automatically inherit $50,000 in equity to be used for down payments or closing costs. By using the $300,000 figure, the buyer must still come in with his own blood, sweat, and tears in the form of a down payment and closing costs. Lenders like some initial equity to be brought to the table by a buyer.

A year also allows for true market conditions to take hold. Sure, a house might have sold for $500,000 a couple of years ago, but how can that same house only sell for $300,000 now? Is there something wrong with the house or is there something wrong with the market? One full year allows for plenty of time to see whether market trends indicate a declining market or whether, in fact, the buyer did indeed find the deal of a lifetime. But one sale at a single point in time can't indicate a true value, whereas several sales in the same neighborhood over an extended period of time can.

Why is seasoning important? It protects the collateral for the lender, who will then be more willing to make a mortgage loan.

If one were able to use the appraised value of a property immediately, and let's say a home bought for $300,000 was appraised at $400,000, then the borrower could place an equity line or cash-out refinance on the new value. Before seasoning guidelines were issued, lenders found that instead of a $400,000 home, they really had a $300,000 home, and they were now upside down on the property because they had just issued a $100,000 equity loan which the borrowers took.

Types of Refinance Mortgages

There are several different types of refinancing and each addresses one or more particular goal.

Rate Refinancing

The most common type of refinancing is a *rate refinance*. This is where someone wants to replace his current mortgage with a new one that has a lower rate. Makes sense, doesn't it? Few would refinance into a higher rate.

Mortgage rates move about in swings. First they're on an upward trend for a while, then they stabilize, then they move back downward, following national economic trends. We'll discuss in detail how and why mortgage rates move in detail in Chapter 5.

Let's say you first bought your property a couple of years ago and you got a 30-year fixed rate mortgage at 7 percent, and interest rates fell to 6 percent. On a $300,000 mortgage, the difference between 7 percent and 6 percent is $1,995 and $1,798, respectively. By refinancing into a lower rate, you're saving $197 per month.

Term Refinancing

A *term refinance* changes the length of the loan, or its term. A 30-year mortgage has a 30-year term, a 15-year mortgage has a 15-year term, and so on. Mortgage rates can be issued by a mortgage lender in 5-year increments.

A longer term keeps the payments lower than a shorter term. Sometimes, people refinance to a shorter term so they'll save on long-term interest charges, while others refinance to a longer term to make their payments more affordable.

If you have a 15-year fixed-rate mortgage and would like to reduce the payments a little, you can opt for a 20-year, 25-year, 30-year, or even longer term mortgage. On a $200,000 15-year loan at 6 percent, the monthly payment would be $1,687. Changing the term to a 30-year loan at 6 percent, the payment drops to $1,199. On the other hand, if you want to shorten the term, a term refinance will change your term from a 30-year to a 20-year, or whatever term you choose. A 30-year loan at 6 percent on $200,000 is $1,199, while 6 percent on a 20-year note ends up being $1,432.

Rate-and-Term Refinancing

A *rate-and-term refinance* is perhaps the most common of the refinances, changing both the rate and/or the term at the same time.

Sometimes, a 30-year loan is 4 or 5 years old, meaning there are 25 or 26 years left to pay. When refinancing to get a lower rate, refinancing into a term similar to the remaining years left can be something to consider, instead of paying even more interest over the long term by starting all over with a brand new 30-year loan. Rate-and-term refinance loans allow rolling closing costs into the loan, and even things such as property tax and insurance can be rolled into the loan and still be classified as a rate-and-term refinance.

Cash-Out Refinancing

A *cash-out refinance* means pulling equity out of your property in the form of cash to you, in addition to replacing the current mortgage. It's important to distinguish between a rate-and-term and a cash-out, because cash-out loans are more expensive than a rate-and-term refinance. Cash-out loans also have restrictions on the amount one can borrow, with most limited to 80 percent of the value of the home.

Let's say you have a house that's worth $400,000, and you have a $200,000 mortgage on it. Rates have dropped from 7 percent to 6.50 percent, and you're going to refinance. While you're at it, you decide you'd like to pull out an additional $20,000 to pay for college or to pay off a car loan. Instead of refinancing $200,000, you're now refinancing $220,000.

Refinancing Multiple Liens

Sometimes, people buy properties with not just one mortgage but with two—one big one and one smaller one. This is often done to avoid *private mortgage insurance,* or *PMI.* PMI is an insurance policy lender's requirement when less than 20 percent is put down on a home purchase. Back more than 50 years ago, many home loans required a hefty down payment on that amount to 20 or 30 percent. That kept a lot of folks who couldn't save up that kind of money out of homes.

But a company called Mortgage Guaranty Insurance Corporation, or MGIC, came up with an insurance policy that would cover the difference between 20 percent down and whatever the buyers put down. If the buyers put 5 percent down, MGIC would issue an insurance policy covering the remaining 15 percent, should the borrowers default. The problem with PMI, though, is that most of the policies are not tax deductible, or at least not those made before 2007.

Multiple liens mean higher rates for mortgages and liens placed in a second or third position. Refinancing multiple liens into one lien gives the homeowner a lower rate. These multiple liens may also be liens placed on the property that aren't loans but judgments awarded third parties who might have sued the homeowner and placed a lien for the awarded amount on the house. The house can never be refinanced or sold without that lien being paid off.

Refinancing an Equity Loan

An *equity loan* is typically an adjustable rate mortgage based on a certain percentage of value on the home. Refinancing an equity loan into a first mortgage gives the borrower one lower, typically fixed interest rate.

Most equity loans are adjustable rate mortgages based on the *Wall Street Journal*'s prime rate, and can move up or down throughout the life of the equity line. An *equity line* is like a checking account or credit card, only the amount you can borrow is limited to the value of the home and your available equity. When you refinance an equity line, you can refinance it by itself or roll it in with a first mortgage to pay it off.

Refinancing Home Improvement Loans

A *home improvement loan* is used to upgrade or remodel a house and is almost always fixed and almost always in a second position. Like other second liens, they carry a higher rate and can be rolled into a first mortgage when refinancing. A major home improvement, such as adding square footage or another roof, would be considered a construction loan. A *construction loan* is also short term, as it only lasts until the construction is completed. At the end of construction, a permanent mortgage must replace the construction note by refinancing.

Refinancing Investment Properties

Financing investment properties with a refinance means higher rates and loan limits, when compared to primary residences. Rates for investment properties are typically 1/4 to 3/8 percent higher. Refinancing investment properties also requires a minimum equity amount, most often 10 percent. An investment refinance loan must then be no more than 90 percent of the value of the property.

Note Modification

A *note modification* is not a refinance in the traditional sense, but it does bear mention because it changes the rate of a mortgage loan, only not with an official refinance.

A note can be modified to a new lower rate by the lender who originally issued the first mortgage. Fees for a modification are minor. When a lender modifies a note, the borrower can't expect the absolute best rates available. The lender knows that a refinance will take some time and effort, so instead of offering their best rate, they might offer something in between. For instance, if you have an 8 percent rate, and market rates are at 7 percent, then you might get a 7.50 percent rate offered to you. If you want to take that rate and not refinance, go ahead. Hey, there's nothing to stop you from refinancing a modified note if rates continue to move downward.

Note modifications are the most cost-effective way to reduce an interest rate, but they can only be done by the original lender, and they can't be done at all if the note has been sold by one lender to another.

A Streamline

A *streamline* is a feature of a government loan, which is one that is backed by the federal government by way of the Department of Housing and Urban Development for an FHA loan, or the Department of Veterans Affairs for a VA loan.

For an FHA loan, the streamline refinance requires that the loan to be refinanced must already be an FHA loan and can't be a cash-out loan; it must only be a rate-and-term. The current FHA loan also cannot be delinquent, and the refinance must lower the monthly payment. An FHA streamline requires almost no paperwork, other than a loan application. An appraisal is rarely required, and there are no credit or income checks the lender needs to perform. As with any other refinance, there are closing costs. If the borrower wants to roll closing costs into the mortgage loan, then an appraisal must be performed. A new refinance loan offered by the FHA is called an *FHA Secure Refinance*. It lets homeowners who have adjustable-rate mortgages that have adjusted to a rate higher than they can pay refinance into an FHA loan with lower rates.

A VA streamline operates in much the same way as an FHA streamline, in that the paperwork is reduced, and there is no need for an appraisal or for credit or income checks, as long as the interest rate is being reduced and also refinanced into a fixed-rate mortgage. A VA streamline refinance is called an *IRRRL*, or an *Interest Rate Reduction Refinance Loan*. (For brevity—if there is such a thing for government projects—it's also called an *IRRL* in public circles, or an *Interest Rate Reduction Loan*.)

Foreclosure Bailout

A *foreclosure bailout* is a rare loan and a type of refinance mortgage that helps people who have gotten behind on their mortgage to refinance out of the old mortgage that is in the process of foreclosing on them, due to missed payments.

When someone applies for a foreclosure bailout, the new loan amount has to cover the old mortgage balance, back interest

and penalties, closing costs, and attorney fees. While a foreclosure bailout is a messy proposition, it can be used when someone does not want to lose his home and has recovered his ability
to repay a mortgage. Foreclosure bailouts require much higher
rates, usually 56 percent above market, low debt-to-income ratios, and a 35–40 percent equity position.

Comparing Cash-Out and Rate-and-Term Refinances

Cash-out refinances can carry slightly higher fees, and loan
amounts are limited to lower *loan-to-values* (LTVs) than a rate-
and-term refinance. Often, this additional fee is 1/4 point in additional charges, meaning that on a $400,000 loan, a cash-out
fee might be $1,000. Other states with more stringent cash-out
requirements, such as Texas, might add even more to the
charges.

There are more restrictive LTV requirements. Whereas cash-
out LTVs are limited to 90 percent of the value of the property
(80 percent in Texas), rate-and-term refinances can go higher
than that. A rate-and-term refinance will only include the current
loan balance plus any accrued interest, closing costs incurred in
the refinance, and any escrow or impound accounts. Again, except for Texas, one can typically receive less than 1 percent of the
loan amounts as cash back at closing and still call it a rate-and-
term refinance without the additional restrictions that cash-out
loans have.

Rescission Period

One feature a refinance has that no other loan has is a *rescission
period*—a three-day time frame after closing papers have been

signed and before the loan can officially fund. It's nothing more than a "cooling off" period to allow you to re-think your refinance loan and make sure you really, really want to do it.

Let's say you got a cash-out loan and you lowered your monthly payment just a little bit, but you also got enough money to pay off a couple of automobile loans and all of your credit balances. You thought about it and thought about it, and finally the loan officer talked you into taking the cash-out loan, and not just a simple rate-and-term refinance. You had wondered throughout the approval process if the loan officer was really acting in your best interest or was simply trying to increase the loan amount so she could get a bigger commission check. Nevertheless, you decided to go ahead and close. At the closing table, you sign a piece of paper called a *rescission notice,* which explains the rescission process. You have three business days—including Saturday—before this loan will officially close. If you change your mind during that time, you simply have to fax or email the lender of your desire to cancel the loan.

Even while you were at the closing table, you were still wondering if this was a smart thing to do, but then realized you had three days to think it over before everything became official. So you signed your papers, took your copies home, and reviewed them over the weekend.

After a couple of days of contemplation, you made up your mind: if you were refinancing to pay off some cars and credit card balances, it was wiser to go ahead and pay off the cars early and the credit cards off completely, without adding more debt to your mortgage. The monthly savings on your new mortgage will help pay off those cars and credit cards quicker, and you won't be financing them over the next 30 years with your new 30-year mortgage.

On Monday, you sign your rescission papers and fax them back to the settlement agent, who will then cancel the loan for you. You don't even need to have a reason. You can say you're canceling because your baseball team lost last night. It doesn't matter. Or you can have a darned good reason for rescinding: your interest rate wasn't what was quoted to you by your loan officer, or the closing costs are sky-high. You name it, you can use it.

A common question comes up when people do rescind: "Do I owe everybody money if I cancel my loan?" No. Lenders might charge a loan-processing fee or an underwriting fee, but if the loan doesn't close, you don't have to pay for it. The same thing goes for attorney or settlement fees—if the loan rescinds, you walk away without being responsible for all those charges.

• CHAPTER TWO •

Why Refinance?

Okay, now that you know about the various types of refinance loans in the marketplace, the question remains, *Should you refinance at all?* After all, there are closing costs in a refinance loan, just as there are in a purchase loan (we'll discuss closing costs in detail in Chapter 6), and loan officers certainly want to make a commission, so they may be inclined to convince you to refinance your mortgage (we'll look at finding the best loan officer in Chapter 4). But the bottom line is that you need to understand how to determine whether refinancing is in your very best interest. No pun intended.

It seems that when rates begin to go down, there's always some mortgage company advertising on the radio, the television, in the newspaper, on the Internet, and even on street corners. "Refinance now, while rates are low!" Mortgage companies spend a lot of money advertising to get you to call them. And given the opportunity, there just might be a sales pitch that will get you to refinance, regardless of your situation. There are sales managers at most mortgage companies who train their loan officers in how to handle objections and how to answer this question or that question when you discuss refinancing with them. But don't let a sales pitch be your guide.

There are a number of factors that you should consider when determining whether refinancing your mortgage is appropriate for you. With this knowledge, you should be able to find out on your own whether refinancing is a good move. Just as there were different types of refinances, there are also different reasons to refinance, along with different motivations—or lack of—for doing so. We'll look at several scenarios and see how you can come to your own conclusion, without being talked into it by some commission-based loan officer.

When to Refinance into a Different Rate

This age-old question has been around for decades, and its mythical answer has always been: "Wait until your interest rate is at least 2 percent lower, before you refinance."

Have you heard that one before? The "2 percent rule" came about because of a few factors, but it was primarily due to the amount of closing costs involved, as well as high interest rates from previous decades. Refinancing with $10,000 worth of closing costs or reducing an interest rate from 18 percent to 17.50 percent didn't make a whole lot of sense. It still doesn't, as a matter of fact. That used to be the "golden rule of thumb" for refinancing. Tell that thumb to take a hike.

Refinancing into a different rate first assumes that the reason to refinance is to get a lower payment. After all, why refinance into a higher rate or with a higher monthly payment, right? You'll know when it might be the time to consider a refinance when you hear news about rates going lower, or that the Federal Reserve Board is meeting and deciding to lower rates, or some such thing.

One of the main considerations of a refinance is that of closing costs. Closing costs are a factor when determining whether or not to refinance and *at what rate*. But how much are closing costs, and who charges them? Yes, there are closing costs and, yes, they can get expensive. In fact, most closing costs you incurred when you purchased the property will also need to be paid during a refinance. In addition, you'll probably need a new appraisal (unless you get a waiver), a new credit report, title insurance, and a host of lender fees and attorney fees. Most everything will show up again on your closing statement.

Let's say you could drop your monthly payment by $50. Would it be worth it to refinance? If your closing costs added up to $8,000, would you refinance if you'd only save $50 per month? Probably not. Would you refinance if your closing costs added up to $8,000 and your monthly savings were $1,000 per month? Probably so. That's the dynamic of closing costs. Costs, as well as rate, play an important role.

The way to decide whether or not it's a good thing to refinance is to take your monthly savings and divide those savings into your closing cost total: that is the number of months required to "recover" your closing fees, as a result of your new monthly payment. So, $8,000 divided by $50-per-month savings is 160 months. That's 13 years. A refinance is a bad idea, in this instance. But $8,000 divided by $1,000-per-month savings is 8 months. A refinance is probably a good idea.

Let's look at a few examples of how costs and rate can help you decide whether or not to refinance your loan, using a 30-year fixed-rate mortgage as your guide.

Current mortgage balance	$100,000
Current rate	7%
Current payment	$665
Closing costs	$3,000
New rate available	6.75%
New payment available	$648
Difference in payment	$17
Months to recover	176 ($3,000 / $17)
Good idea?	No

Okay, now let's make an adjustment by changing one element—the rates.

Current mortgage balance	$100,000
Current rate	7.75%
Current payment	$716
Closing costs	$3,000
New rate available	6.25%
New payment available	$615
Difference in payment	$101
Months to recover	29 ($3,000 / $101)
Good idea?	Yes

There's sometimes a question about how many months are ideal to recover closing costs, and there's no definite answer. Is 29 months okay, but not 30 months? Or is 18 months good, but not 29 months? I would say that a good time frame would be something less than 48 months, or 4 years. The fewer, the better. But in most cases, you simply need to own the property for at least as long as it takes to recover your fees.

Now let's take that same interest rate refinance scenario and again adjust another element: the mortgage amount.

Current mortgage balance	$500,000
Current rate	7.75%
Current payment	$3,582
Closing costs	$3,000
New rate available	6.25%
New payment available	$3,078
Difference in payment	$504
Months to recover	6 ($3,000 / $504)
Good idea?	You'd better believe it

Why the huge difference in months to recover? The difference is caused by the increase in the amount borrowed. The greater the amount of the loan, the more effect the rate change will have on your final monthly payment.

There are fixed costs in refinancing and there are those that are dependent on the rate. Title insurance, for instance, will be higher, along with the loan amount, but other costs that are fixed—attorney fees, escrow fees, closing fees, appraisal charges, and document preparation—do not change. The smaller the amount of the loan, the greater these fixed costs represent as a percentage, when compared to the loan.

For instance, a $300 appraisal is 1 percent of a small loan of $30,000. Add an attorney's charge of $200, a closing fee of $200, and throw in a new $500 survey, and those fixed charges add up to $1,200, or 4 percent of the loan amount of $30,000. Now compare those same fixed costs of $1,200 to a loan of $500,000, and the result is only 0.2 percent. The larger the loan, the less costs will affect the equation. This makes closing cost recovery time quicker.

Now let's go back to the original example and test that theory.

Current mortgage balance	$500,000
Current rate	7%
Current payment	$3,326
Closing costs	$3,000
New rate available	6.75%
New payment available	$3,242
Difference in payment	$84
Months to recover	35 ($3,000 / $84)
Good idea?	Probably—as long as you own the property for at least 35 months

Did you see the effect that costs and the amount of the loan have on a transaction? If the new rate was just another ¹/₄ percent lower than 6.75 percent (at 6.50 percent), then the monthly savings would be $166, making the recovery time just 18 months. With larger loans, the $3,000 closing cost figure will be higher due to non-fixed costs, such as title insurance or origination charges, but this number remains the same and helps to explain how to properly calculate recovery.

Let's look at another variation on this theme: the age of the current mortgage. We'll begin by reviewing the initial example:

Current mortgage balance	$100,000
Current rate	7%

Current payment	$665
Closing costs	$3,000
New rate available	6.75%
New payment available	$648
Difference in payment	$17
Months to recover	176 ($3,000 / $17)
Good idea?	No

In this case, the current mortgage balance is the benchmark for both the current and future rate. However, the current mortgage balance is based on the original mortgage balance, not the balance on which the current rate is based. When you bought the property and came in with your down payment money, your loan was based on the initial amount borrowed. Let's say you bought a house for $150,000, put 20 percent down, and your original loan was $120,000. At 7 percent on a 30-year mortgage of $120,000, the scenario would look like this:

Original mortgage balance	$120,000
Current mortgage balance	$100,000
Current rate	7%
Current payment	$798 (based on $120,000)
Closing costs	$3,000
New rate available	6.75%
New payment available	$648 (based on $100,000)
Difference in payment	$150
Months to recover	20 ($3,000 / $150)
Good idea?	Yes

In the initial example, with the difference in rate being only .25 percent (from 7 percent to 6.75 percent), it would take 13 years to recover the costs. But because the amount of the loan changed along with the rate, the recovery period changed dramatically.

The interest rate refinance is the simplest form of refinance, yet it shows the various factors involved when making a decision. Changing the rate and loan amount, either together or independently, can affect your decision. But by using this method to help determine "why" or "why not" you should refinance your loan for another rate, you can simplify the method. Forget the old 2 percent rule. There are times when it might be an opportune time to refinance, in order to get a higher rate or payment. It's not going to happen often, but there can be instances where one could consider it, and it involves increasing the rate to get a lower payment.

How can that be?

Refinancing the Term

Mortgage loans can be amortized, or *paid out,* over almost any agreed-upon time frame, but lenders typically keep those time frames from 10 to 40 years, in increments of 5 years.

Loans can be set for 10, 15, 20, 25, 30, 35, or 40 years. Some lenders offer 50-year loans, but I haven't seen many of them, nor have I seen many 35-year loans. What happens when you change the term of the loan? Your payment can go up or it can go down, but the shorter the term, the higher the monthly payment. The longer the term, the lower the payment. By "squishing" the amount borrowed into a shorter period, the payments will be higher, even though the rate will be lower with a shorter term.

On a $300,000 loan over 15 years at 5 percent, the payment is $2,372, while the payment on $300,000 over 30 years at 5.25 percent is $1,656. The rate on a 30-year mortgage goes up, but because the time to pay it all back is twice as long, the payment is actually lower.

It's easy to understand this difference by comparing it to a 2-year fixed loan (which doesn't actually exist) on $300,000. At 3 percent (a lower rate), you'd have to make 24 payments of $12,894 per month. Yes, the rate is lower, but because the term is shorter, the payments skyrocket. Why do a term refinance? To either decrease monthly payments or to amortize a loan to a pre-set point in the future.

I recall a client who contacted me for a refinance loan. He had a 30-year mortgage but wanted a 15-year mortgage. His payment would actually go up, and his scenario looked like this:

Current mortgage balance	$300,000 (with 27 years left)
Current rate	6%
Current payment	$1,798
Closing costs	$3,000
New rate available	5.75%
New payment available	$2,498
Difference in payment	($693)
Months to recover	None
Good idea?	Yes

Excuse me? He loses $693, and it's a good idea? In his case, you'd better believe it. But why did he want to refinance in the first place, to increase his payment? Yes, he would save on interest paid over the life of the loan by paying interest at a lower rate over a shorter period with a 15-year fixed-rate loan, but he had another reason.

> "My daughter is two years old, and in 15 years she'll be heading to college. I want to have my mortgage paid off when she goes to school, so that's why I'm refinancing," he said.
>
> "Then you could simply prepay the mortgage anytime you wanted, instead of refinancing, couldn't you?" I asked.
>
> "Yes, I could. But I want the payment to come out automatically from my checking account each month. Sometimes I may not have the discipline to make extra payments on a 30-year loan. I just want it to be on auto-pilot."

It made perfect sense. He admitted that he may not have had the financial discipline to make extra payments, but wanted to be mortgage-free in 15 years. A term refinance fulfilled his requirement, and he was comfortable with the higher payments.

Here's an opposite twist: changing the term to reduce the payment.

A couple originally took out a mortgage loan. Wanting to pay it off sooner rather than later, they took out a 10-year mortgage loan. Plans changed soon thereafter when the wife became pregnant. She didn't want to work while raising their baby, so they would only be operating on one income rather than the two they used to qualify for the higher payment on a 10-year note. Their scenario looked this way:

Current mortgage balance	$200,000
Current rate	6% (on a 10-year mortgage)

Current payment	$2,220
Closing costs	$3,000
New rate available	6.25% (on a 30-year mortgage)
New payment available	$1,231
Difference in payment	$989 (that's a lot of diapers)
Months to recover	3 ($3,000 / $989)
Good idea?	Yes

By increasing the rate but significantly increasing their term, their payment dropped nearly in half. Yes, they would have to pay more in long-term interest if they kept to the 30-year repayment schedule, but most mortgage loans allow for people to pay ahead on their mortgage, or "prepay," so they could still keep on their 10-year payoff schedule but at their own leisure, by sending in extra money each month to pay their mortgage down.

When refinancing into a different term, it's important to remember that the longer the term, the more interest you'll pay. For example, this chart will show how much you'll pay in interest over the life of a loan, based upon the same initial loan amount of $200,000:

Term (Years)	Rate	Payment	Interest Paid
10	6%	$2,220	$ 66,449
15	6%	$1,687	$103,660
20	6%	$1,432	$143,680
25	6.25%	$1,319	$195,801
30	6.25%	$1,231	$243,160
40	6.25%	$1,135	$344,800

You can see how much of a difference the term alone makes when refinancing. And it's vital that you consider the long-term effects of long mortgage terms. Not everyone can afford a 10-

year loan, compared to a 40-year term. Sometimes, people can only get qualified with lower payments, hence the longer term. Say there's a home you really, really want to buy, but you can't afford a $2,220-per-month payment. And say you can easily handle a $1,231 payment. Which do you choose? If it's a case of wanting to qualify for the loan, then take whatever you can qualify for. But just because the 40-year term looks more appealing on a monthly basis, it can harm you because the mortgage loan balance takes longer to pay down.

Now let's look at what the mortgage balance would be under the very same scenario, after 10 years:

Term (Years)	Rate	Payment	Interest Paid	Balance after 10 Years
10	6%	$2,220	$ 66,449	-0-
15	6%	$1,687	$103,660	$ 87,297
20	6%	$1,432	$143,680	$129,062
25	6.25%	$1,319	$195,801	$153,872
30	6.25%	$1,231	$243,160	$168,475
40	6.25%	$1,135	$344,800	$184,415

Amazing isn't it? By taking a 40-year loan, you've only paid the balance down by $15,585 after 10 years of mortgage payments. So, is there a secret rule? I think so, but it's still a subjective one: take the shortest term you're most comfortable with, and make extra payments along the way. If you structure your loan term in that fashion, you'll pay your note down sooner at a rate you feel good about, paying extra on your note all the while, whenever you want.

Choosing the wrong term can cost you thousands and thousands of dollars. Sure, there are those who say, "But David, you can write off that mortgage interest so you're losing that larger deduction!" And yes, that's true. But in reality, when you "write off" mortgage interest, you're only deducting the interest paid from your taxable income. You don't deduct $184,415 from your income tax liability; you're only deducting the mortgage interest you paid from your gross income. If you're in the 29 percent tax rate, then that's what you can deduct from your income for tax purposes. But you're still hit with the other interest expense you paid at 71 percent.

In fact, if that logic of getting an interest deduction made complete sense, then why not refinance to a rate of 20 percent? Or 25 percent to get the higher deduction? It doesn't take much to figure that one out, does it?

Adjusting the Term to Fit Your Payment

Mortgage payments are calculated using four basic functions:

1. Term (the number of months to pay off the loan)

2. Interest rate

3. Amount financed

4. Payment

In this fashion, it's how monthly payments are calculated. If you know the term, the rate, and the amount financed, you'll arrive at the payment:

Term	360 months
Interest rate	7%

Amount financed	$100,000
Monthly payment	$665

This math doesn't just work for calculating payments. If you know any of the three functions, you can calculate the fourth. For instance, if you know the payment, term, and amount financed, you can find the interest rate. Let's say you wanted your payment to be no higher than $725 per month and you wanted a 25-year term on $100,000:

Payment	$725
Term	300 months
Amount financed	$100,000
Rate calculates to	7.28%

It's by using this technique of modifying the four parts of your mortgage calculation to suit your specific requirements that you can change a monthly payment or change the term of your loan.

I recall a woman who wanted to refinance her mortgages—a first mortgage at 7 percent and a second mortgage at 8.50 percent. Rates were lower, so she was investigating refinancing both notes into one lower rate. However, she also had one specific request: she was going to retire in 20 years and did not want to still be paying on her mortgage, so we used the following formula to calculate what her monthly payments and rate should be to accomplish her goal:

Current mortgage payments

First mortgage (30-year fixed)	$200,000	7%	$1,330
Second mortgage (30-year fixed)	$ 40,000	8.50%	$ 307
Total payments			$1,637

*New mortgage plan to retire in **20 years***

Term	240 months
Amount financed	$240,000
Interest rate	6.75%
New monthly payment	$1,824

Could she have gotten a lower payment? Sure, she could have selected a 30- or 40-year term, and the payments would have been lower. But that wasn't her goal.

You can't *always* get what you want, though. Your goals may not match what's available in the current market. Just because you want 6.75 percent on a 30-year fixed doesn't mean it's available (we'll discuss how interest rates are set in Chapter 6). Let's say this woman wanted to be mortgage-free in 20 years, but wanted her payment to be no higher than $1,500 per month. By knowing three of the four components, we can find the fourth:

Term	240 months
Amount financed	$240,000
New monthly payment	$1,500
New interest rate	4.35%

As you can see, although she wanted to be able to pay off the note in 20 years and have a payment no higher than $1,500 per month, she won't be able to achieve her goals. Rates have never been that low. It's not impossible that rates would ever get to 4.35 percent, but the point is that just because you have a particular requirement, it doesn't mean it can be met.

Reasons to Refinance

Refinancing to Change the Rate or Term

A *rate-and-term refinance* is really a combination of the two forms of refinancing we've discussed. In fact, you may hear about the rate-and-term refinance more often than you hear of a rate refinance or a term refinance. Often, though, you are refinancing for a lower rate and likely keeping it on the same loan term. Even if you currently have a 30-year mortgage and you're refinancing into another 30-year mortgage, you're still changing the term because you're probably 2, 3, or more years into your current note. This is why you'll usually hear of rate-and-term and *cash-out* as the two types of refinancing.

Refinancing to Consolidate Debt or Cash Out

This is the infamous cash-out refinance you've heard about, and the one with the most advertising: "Refinance now to get a new lower rate!" or "Cash out your equity!"

But a cash-out refinance needs to be evaluated even further, if you want to make the right financial decisions. Not only do you need to make all the same considerations regarding a rate-and term-refinance, but you also need to understand how pulling equity out of your home will impact your monthly payments, interest rate, and term. Why pull out cash? There are as many reasons as there are stars in the sky, it seems, but that cash comes from your equity in your home, and that equity can come from:

- Making extra payments toward your principal balance

- Property appreciation

When you make more than your regular payment, or a prepayment, you're paying down your note and building equity at a faster clip. Let's say you bought a house for $500,000 and put 20 percent down, giving you a $400,000 mortgage. You immediately have a 20 percent equity position. After 5 years with a 15-year fixed mortgage at 6 percent, your principal balance would have been paid down to $304,036. You now have $500,000— $304,036 = $195,964 in equity.

Let's now say that each month, you add in an extra $100 to go toward principal. This extra $100 over 5 years brings your note even lower, to $297,059. You now have $500,000 − $297,059 = $202,941 in equity. If property values appreciate, your equity position will grow even further. Let's assume a 10 percent annual increase in property values for that same period. After 5 years, your property would be worth $805,255. If you also prepaid that same $100 per month, you now have $805,255 − $297,059 = $508,196 in equity. It's the $508,196 that's available for you to "tap into," at least up to lending guidelines that may allow only up to 90 percent of the value of the home to be taken out as equity. But it's generally advised not to borrow that much, as higher rates and PMI come into play, when borrowing more than 75 percent of the value of the property.

If you wanted to cash-out refinance your mortgage up to 75 percent of the value of the home, the results would look like this:

$805,255 value × 75 percent = $603,941
$603,941 − $297,059 mortgage balance = $306,882
available equity

That's a cash-out refinance.

What can you pay off? Mostly anything you want. Common cash-out refinances pay off credit cards, automobile payments, and student loans. And they are a relatively cheap way to do so, especially when compared to the monthly payments and rates found on most credit card accounts and auto loans. A mortgage rate at 6 percent is much lower than a credit card rate at 18 percent, right? Besides, mortgage interest is tax deductible, whereas interest on a credit card is not. But you need to understand the impact of cashing out to pay off debt, because the initial math is alluring and makes for an easy sales pitch from a loan officer.

Let's look at a couple of examples:

Current mortgage (30-year fixed-rate at 7 percent)

Mortgage balance	$200,000
Monthly payment	$1,330

Current consumer debt:

Automobile payment	$709
Balance	$35,000
Credit card payments	$350
Balance	$15,000

So the loan officer says, "Hey, I noticed you've got a couple of credit cards and an automobile loan. What do you say I run some numbers to see if it might be a good idea to do a cash-out refinance and pay off those loans?" To begin with, the payments will always be lower, because you're spreading out the loan balance over 30 years. If a loan officer says this to you, understand that he's not really going to do some arduous algebraic calculations to figure this one out; it's just part of the pitch.

But let's continue. If 30-year mortgage rates are at 6.75 percent or .25 percent lower than your current 7 percent, if you only did a rate-and-term, the new monthly payments would be:

Term	360 months
Interest rate	6.75%
Amount financed	$200,000
Monthly payment	$1,297

What's the recovery period? It's $3,000 / $33 = 91 months. Is this a good idea? No. When you add the car payment of $709 and the credit card payments of $350, the total monthly payments are:

Mortgage	$1,297
Auto	$709
Credit cards	$350
Total monthly payments	$2,356

Then the telephone rings, and it's that loan officer who wants to help you reduce your monthly payments, and I'll just bet he's found a way to save you lots of money. "If you did a cash-out refinance and paid off your car loan and credit cards while lowering your rate to 6.75 percent, then you'll save $735 per month! I'll send the paperwork over right away!"

And he's right, because you rolled your current mortgage, car loan, and credit card debt into one note at 6.75 percent. Of course it works out.

Current mortgage	$200,000
Auto loan	$35,000
Credit cards	$15,000
Total debt	$250,000

New mortgage

Term	360 months
Interest rate	6.75%
Amount financed	$250,000
Monthly payment	$1,621

Because you paid off your consumer debt along with your mortgage, your total monthly payments drop from $2,356 to $1,621. Is this a good idea? Maybe. You've just lowered your monthly debt with tax-deductible mortgage interest, but you've also increased the long-term cost of your automobile and credit cards.

If you borrowed $35,000 over 60 months at 8 percent, you would have paid $7,580 in interest. By including that same $35,000 in a new mortgage at 6.75 percent over 30 years, you would pay $46,723 in interest over the life of the loan, not to mention the $3,000 in closing costs required to close the deal. On an annual basis, the additional interest is palpable at around $1,500 on average. And yes, there is the increased tax deduction, but understand that when you cash-out refinance, you're significantly increasing the interest paid over time.

The credit card payments also drop to $97 per month when rolled into the mortgage, compared to the $350 paid each month at 18 percent. And what if you decide you'd like to charge those credit cards back up again to the original $15,000 balance? Then you might have done more harm than good. Paying off credit accounts really doesn't do much if you charge those accounts right back up again. In fact, you've made the situation worse by incurring still more debt and eating into the equity in your home. If you pay off credit cards with a cash-out refinance, you should keep those cards at a zero balance each month and not let that debt accumulate.

Okay, okay. I know that people don't keep a mortgage for 30 years, so the long-term interest on the automobile and credit card loans won't ever reach that level, but the fact remains that it's likely you'll be paying much more in interest over however long your cash-out refinance remains on the books.

When should you do a cash-out refinance? All things being equal, I suggest a cash-out refinance if you were going to do a rate-and-term refinance anyway. If rates have dropped enough that your recovery period is acceptable under a rate-and-term, then why not take a look at a cash-out refinance? This is because closing costs are involved, and if you simply want to pay off a car and some credit cards with your equity, then take out an equity loan instead.

Equity loans are second mortgages at a slightly higher rate than what's available for first mortgages, but they're cheap in relation to closing costs for a first mortgage. How cheap? Most banks that offer equity loans give them to you for free, as long as you tap into the equity at least once per year. If your recovery period doesn't pass the test for a rate-and-term and you'd still like to pay off that car and those credit cards, look at an equity loan. You may find some resistance from your loan officer, though, if that's what you decide because, after all, loan officers make more money on bigger first mortgages and little —if any— money on equity loans. But if you follow this advice, you'll make the correct decision.

Refinancing to Remove Someone from the Loan

Sometimes people buy property together and then, one day, one of them decides he wants out. This could be a business partner, a family member, or a spouse, and he or she might want to "cash in" their chips and move on, or, in the case of a divorce, one of the spouses may want to keep the house, while the other wants nothing whatsoever to do with it.

When multiple individuals buy property together, they all have a legal interest in and rights to the property that go along with owning real estate. This interest is evidenced by a *title report*, which shows every legal entity that has some sort of claim of ownership in the property.

If a married couple buys a house together, they will both be recorded as having an ownership in the property. If that couple get a gift from their parents to help buy the home, but the parents don't appear on the mortgage with the couple, they could still appear on the title report if the couple granted them an interest in the property by a document called a *warranty deed*. A warranty deed is a legal instrument that assigns ownership rights in real estate. In this case, the couple would be on the mortgage and the parents would not. But they would all have an ownership interest in the property. If, later on, the couple sells that property to someone else and transfers their ownership to the new buyers, again by way of a warranty deed, that still leaves Mom and Dad on the title. That means the new buyers won't be able to get financing on the property until Mom and Dad agree to be removed from the title report along with their children who sold the home. Even though Mom and Dad aren't on the mortgage, they have a legal and recorded interest in the property that must be addressed before any future liens can be placed on the property.

Sometimes, when a couple buys a home and gets divorced, one spouse wants to keep the house, or the house may be awarded to one spouse by the divorce court. But the spouse who moves out is still on the title and is still obligated to pay the mortgage. Until the ex who remains in the house refinances the mortgage and the ex who moved out signs a warranty deed relinquishing all claims to the property, the ex will always be on the mortgage and title until the property is sold and the process starts all over again. Regardless of what a divorce court says, the lender couldn't care less if the courts said the husband, for example, had to give the house to the wife and that he's no longer responsible for repaying the loan. That's simply not true. When the lender originally made the loan to the previously happily married couple, both their incomes were used to qualify them. It's not the lender's fault that the marriage went awry. The lender still wants its money, regardless of the divorce settlement.

The ex-husband who moved and believes he doesn't have to pay the mortgage could find himself in trouble if he doesn't get taken off the mortgage. And this can only be done by a refinance. It's to the ex-husband's benefit to be taken off of the mortgage. Otherwise, the mortgage payment will show up on his credit report and be counted as part of his debt load. That could hamper his qualification efforts if he tries to buy a new home. He would have to qualify while carrying two mortgage payments. The spouse who *does* stay in the property and refinances to get the ex off title and the mortgage must now qualify on her own, with just one income. If she can't, she'll have to enlist the services of a co-borrower to qualify, sell the house, or do nothing—in which case, her ex will remain on the note.

This situation would work just fine, unless the court orders her to refinance to get him off of the mortgage. If she can't, she may have to sell the property. Just like a divorced couple, business partners who part ways may also have to refinance on their own to get a former partner off the mortgage and title.

Refinancing to Remove Private Mortgage Insurance (PMI)

On loans with less than 20 percent down, there is often a *private mortgage insurance* policy, or *PMI,* and depending on when the property was purchased, that PMI payment may or may not be tax deductible. If it's not tax deductible, you can refinance to get that policy off your monthly payment.

A typical PMI payment is about .50 percent of the loan amount, divided by 12. PMI payments will vary depending on whether the buyer puts in more or less cash. Payments may also vary based on the type of loan being insured (fixed or adjustable, for example), or on whether the borrowers have less-than-perfect credit.

If you bought a $200,000 home a couple of years ago with 10 percent down, your first mortgage would be 90 percent of $200,000, or $180,000, and you would have a PMI payment as well. If a 30-year fixed-rate was at 6.50 percent, the principal and interest payment on $180,000 would be $1,137, and the PMI payment would be about .50 percent × $180,000 divided by 12 (months), or $75 per month.

If the PMI policy is not tax deductible, at some point after your balance reaches 80 percent of the sales price, you will want to refinance your mortgage to get rid of that payment. You gain equity in the same way as described earlier, with extra payments, price appreciation, or both.

Let's say that after a couple of years, you decide you want a PMI payment off your mortgage. First, ask your loan officer to speak with one of her appraisers about determining the property's value and comparing it with your current mortgage balance. If there's enough value, you would refinance out of the old loan and into the new one without the PMI.

Refinancing Multiple Liens

A lien on a property doesn't have to be a mortgage loan, and you can certainly have more than one mortgage loan, say a first and second used to buy the property. But other liens can show up on the property as well—such as a mechanic's lien, filed on a property when a building contractor begins some type of remodeling or construction work. If the remodeling loan was never paid off, the contractor would leave the lien on there until it was paid in full.

When there are existing liens on a property prior to a refinance, those existing liens take priority over a new refinance loan, meaning that the existing liens would agree to subordinate to the new mortgage or would have to be paid off entirely. *Subor-*

dinating to a new mortgage means agreeing to take a second or third position behind a first mortgage.

Often, a mechanic's lien is left on the property due to a dispute. Maybe the owners didn't agree on the quality of the work or there was a dispute on the contract. I've seen mechanics' liens where the contractor simply walked off of the job. A lien can also be placed on a property for unpaid property taxes or unpaid income taxes. In some states, a lien can be placed on a property for bad consumer loans or collection accounts.

Refinancing multiple liens will require getting payoff information, such as the amount requested—with any accrued interest—from each and every lien holder. At closing, each lien holder will receive his funds from the refinance and will sign a warranty deed or *release of lien* absolving him of any future interest.

Refinancing to Avoid Foreclosure

Sometimes, bad things happen. People can lose their jobs or suddenly become ill and unable to work. Economies can change and factories can close, leaving people without a regular source of income, sapping their savings.

When someone can't pay his mortgage, the lender takes steps to take the property back. How does a foreclosure happen? Normally, foreclosures happen when a property owner misses three payments in a row. Then the wheels begin to turn, and the lender begins the foreclosure process.

Once a loan goes into the foreclosure process, the property owner has the opportunity to make up for the lost payments and reinstate the mortgage. This reinstatement amount will include the past due payments, plus the next payment, plus any attorney and collection charges. That's a lot, and if the property owner couldn't make a *regular* payment, how could he make the equivalent of four payments plus attorney fees?

Many times, people get behind because they're out of work, yet after soon finding work, they still don't have enough to pay everything off. They might be able to make a regular monthly payment again but don't yet have the financial wherewithal to come up with all that past due money in time to stave off a foreclosure.

There are mortgages available called *foreclosure bailouts* that allow a property owner to refinance the note, along with any past due mortgage payments or attorney and collection fees. Let's say that on a $200,000 mortgage with payments of $1,330 per month, 4 months' interest is required to reinstate the mortgage. That comes to $5,320 plus attorney and collection charges of $1,000. So far, that's $6,320.

Now add $3,000 in closing costs, and your payoff would be about $200,000 + $6,320 + $3,000 = $209,320. Voila! No more foreclosure!

Sounds like a simple enough cure, but this medicine may cause severe side-effects.

First, foreclosure bailouts are a form of subprime lending. Subprime mortgages are made to those whose credit is less than

prime. If you have had recent credit problems, such as late payments or collection accounts, and can't qualify for a conventional
or government loan, then subprime loans can come into play
and provide financing for you. The drawback is that subprime
loans require both higher rates and more equity. And foreclosure
bailouts are considered to be the riskiest of all mortgage loans to
be made. A foreclosure bailout mortgage will determine why
you're suddenly able to pay the new mortgage and not the old.

If one can show that he makes regular payments yet can't
pay off the entire amount due before the foreclosure, then a foreclosure bailout might be in the picture. A foreclosure bailout is
the refinance of last resort, but there are a few lenders who offer
this product.

Renovation/Refinance Loans

This is a relatively new type of loan that allows you to remodel
your home and refinance your mortgage at the same time. The
benefit is that you get the best rate available for a standard refinance, and you get that same great rate for the construction
work.

Typically, construction loans are shorter-term, covering just
the construction period alone; they are adjustable mortgages as
well, usually based on prime. We'll discuss different loan programs in more detail in Chapter 3.

At the end of a construction period, that construction loan
has to be replaced with a permanent, or regular mortgage. That's
when you would have to refinance the construction loan, along

with the standard closing costs attached to the transaction. Adjustable-rate mortgages associated with the prime rate are typically higher than what you can get with a long-term fixed mortgage. If you're thinking of refinancing, you may also want to consider remodeling or renovating your home at the best possible rates.

Let's say your current rate is at 7 percent, and you owe $200,000 on a 30-year mortgage. Your current value is $275,000, or a 72 *loan-to-value ratio (LTV)*, and mortgage rates have dropped to 6.25 percent. You determine that it's a good idea to refinance. But at the same time, what if you have also been thinking of adding on a bedroom and a bath? Typically, you would go to the bank and get a construction loan. But with the refinance/remodel loan, you can kill two birds with one stone.

To complete this type of loan you'll need to get some hard numbers, such as the cost of materials, labor, permits, and all associated costs and fees. First, go to an architect and have her draw up a set of plans. Then take the plans to a builder and ask for a bid; bring your plans and specifications, along with the builder's estimated cost to add on the additional room.

In this example, let's say the additional room will cost an extra $75,000, so you will add in the construction costs with your current loan amount of $200,000, plus closing costs of $3,000, and your new loan balance will be:

$75,000 + $200,000 + $3,000 = $278,000

But wait! Isn't your value only $275,000? Yes, and that gives you a 101 percent LTV! Refinance loans won't let you go that high in terms of loan-to-value, right? With a remodel/refinance loan, there's a twist: the value will be based on the addition's already having been completed, not on the current valuation! That's because the appraiser assigned to value the property will take your blueprints along with the cost estimate and physically visit your property. He'll imagine your new bedroom and bath being complete and he'll determine the value from that standpoint. So, if your home suddenly goes from a two-bedroom home to a three-bedroom home, then your new value could be $325,000, or an 85 percent LTV. That leaves enough room for a refinance with either mortgage insurance or two liens of $260,000 and $18,000.

There are two types of loans designed by Fannie Mae and Freddie Mac, by the way. Fannie Mae's offering is called the *Homestyle* mortgage, and Freddie Mac's version is the *Renovation Plus* loan. There are virtually no differences between the two. Not every lender offers these products; it may take a few phone calls to find one that does. But if you're considering remodeling, you may want to find out if it makes sense to refinance as well. If rates are lower and your recovery period is within guidelines, a remodel/refinance loan can't be beat.

Tangible Net Benefit

This is an analysis to help determine whether a refinance is right for you. Some states have a tangible net benefit law requiring that a refinancing result in a reasonable, tangible net benefit to the borrower, such as a reduced monthly payment.

For example, a tangible net benefit might be that the *annual percentage rate,* or *APR,* cannot exceed 0.5 percent of the initial note rate. In other words, if you're refinancing into a 30-year fixed-rate at 6.25 percent, then the APR can't exceed 6.75 percent of the loan. The APR is defined as the cost of money borrowed, expressed as an annual rate. The cost of money borrowed includes not only the interest rate but certain lender closing costs associated with obtaining that rate, such as appraisal charges and lender fees. We'll discuss APR in more detail in Chapter 6.

Another example of a tangible net benefit: a limit on closing costs associated with obtaining that loan—sort of a back-end way to accomplish the same thing as comparing an APR with a note rate. In some states, under the tangible net benefit law, closing costs can't exceed 0.5 percent of the loan amount.

There is no national tangible net benefit mandate. State laws change with each legislative session, while other states have no tangible net benefit laws at all. But by using your own judgment and adhering to the advice in this book, you can determine on your own whether or not refinancing has a tangible net benefit.

When Not to Refinance

In a nutshell, when it "just doesn't feel right"—when your gut tells you the loan officer is shady or the salesperson is shifty. If this happens, trust your instincts and find another brokerage where you feel more comfortable with the people.

Sometimes, however, you shouldn't refinance under *any* circumstances. Don't refinance from a fixed- to an *adjustable-rate mortgage,* or *ARM,* if the fully indexed rate is higher than your current rate. (We'll discuss ARMs in more detail in Chapter 5.) For now, we'll look at just two components: index and margin.

The *index* is the base number upon which your new rate is set. A common index might be a 1-year Treasury bill. The *margin* is the number added to the index to get your mortgage rate. A common margin might be 2.75 percent.

If a 1-year Treasury bill today is 5 percent and the margin is 2.75 percent, then your new mortgage rate would be 7.75 percent. This new rate is also called the *fully indexed rate* because both the index and margin are added to get your new rate. If fixed rates are at 6 percent, you wouldn't refinance into an ARM. Seems pretty straightforward, right?

Wrong. ARM programs typically have "teaser" rates that are much lower than the fully indexed rate. The teaser rates are offered to entice you into taking an adjustable loan. A teaser rate might be 5 percent, much lower than your fixed rate of 6 percent. If you receive a postcard, an email, or see an advertisement about refinancing to lower rates, keep in mind that even if the rate is below what you currently have, and it's adjustable, it's a trap— one you should avoid.

Avoid the Interest-Only Loan

This is similar to the ARM because it can appear to be attractive, and the pitch from the loan officer can make it doubly so. An *interest-only loan* allows you to make interest-only payments instead of a regular, fully amortized payment. When you make a fully amortized payment on a fixed-rate loan, part of your payment goes to principal and part to interest. With an interest-only loan, only interest is paid. Nothing goes toward principal.

Using $300,000 on a 30-year loan at 7 percent, the principal and interest payment is $1,995. An interest-only payment at 7 percent on $300,000 is $1,775. That's $245 per month and might be something to look at. Yet beware, because in spite of the loan officer's slick pitch, you're never paying down your mortgage.

Don't Churn

Churning is the notion of refinancing over and over again, typically at the behest of a loan officer, and it's usually associated with cashing out some equity while, at the same time, paying off consumer debt or riding interest rates as they fall.

Each time a loan is refinanced, there are costs. Unless property values are increasing each time to cover the refinance costs, you're slowly eating away at your equity by adding to your loan balance. Churning is especially harmful, if each time you do it you pay off consumer debt that you built up since your last refinance.

Remember how easy it is to make a case for refinancing a mortgage while at the same time paying off credit card debt or an automobile loan? Loan officers who target past customers to churn their mortgage know who is most likely to churn and who is not, based on their previous experiences with those customers. People who regularly run up their credit card debt to previous levels can expect a call from their loan officer if mortgage rates are either holding steady or dropping. The loan officer will offer up some "fuzzy math" and pitch how refinancing makes sense. It doesn't.

Still worse is churning into an adjustable rate or interest-only loan. There is absolutely no reason to refinance a loan over and over again, other than to line the pockets of a loan officer.

The Refinance Process in Review

Now that we've got the "what" and the "why" down pat, let's review the refinance process itself.

The refinance process is practically identical to the purchase process. But instead of looking for a down payment, the lender looks for equity in the property.

When you apply for a mortgage loan, your loan application is reviewed through an *Automated Underwriting System*, or *AUS*. Typically, the AUS decision comes back seconds after your loan officer submits the application. The decision will include all the things needed to close your loan. Your loan will be documented with information about you and about the property.

After completing your application, the next step is to provide information about your income and your assets. You will also be introduced to your *loan processor*, who is the person who documents your file and gets it into a position where it complies with the lender's loan guidelines.

Your documentation will include your most recent pay stubs covering 30 days and your most recent three months' worth of bank or investment statements. You will also provide to your loan processor information about who your insurance carrier is so the lender can verify your insurance coverage.

Your loan processor will then contact an attorney or a title company in your area to schedule a closing date and get a copy of your updated title report. Your appraisal, if needed, will also be ordered at this time. Now the ball is *really* rolling, with different people doing different things behind the scenes.

After about a week, your appraisal and title work will most likely have been performed and delivered to your loan processor for review. You also want to tell your loan processor that you want to review the title report and the appraisal, too. When you review a title report, you're looking specifically for a section that lists all current and previous liens, especially if you have a common name such as Joe Smith or Jane Harris. Why?

When other people get behind on their property taxes or their income taxes, or have judgments levied against them by creditors, those tax liens can erroneously show up on your title report. You may not be the only Jane Harris in town. And since title reports do not include Social Security numbers, lien holders may issue a lien on a Jane Harris without verifying *which* Jane Harris! That may not be fair, but that's how it happens. You could find liens filed against your property. If you do, it will be up to you to prove that the Jane Harris on the title report is not you. This is accomplished by having your loan processor, attorney, or title representative get lien reports from the agency that filed them. When that paperwork comes back with the *other* Jane Harris'

Social Security number, you should be able to correct the mistake.

All too often at the very beginning of the loan process, the title report isn't reviewed as carefully as it should be. It can take some time to correct errors, and you may need all the time you can get if you're trying to refinance a mortgage when rates appear to be moving back up.

Take a look at the appraisal as well, so you can see what the appraiser compared to your property in order to arrive at a value. This is important when there might be valuation problems or when properties in your area have been on the decline. An appraiser can only use recorded sales in your area. She may not know about the private transaction next door that brought in $20,000 more than the other comparable sales she used to prepare your appraisal report. If you know of sales in your area that aren't showing up on your appraisal report, it's your obligation to tell the appraiser.

The loan processor will also order tax certificates that document your current tax rate. If there are any past due taxes, they must be paid prior to your closing. The loan processor will also perform other background tasks, such as getting your credit report and ordering flood data on your home to see if the property is located in a flood zone.

Once all your documentation is gathered together, your loan processor will physically or electronically deliver your loan package to the *underwriter*—the person who makes sure that the loan file and documentation meet approval guidelines. Your underwriter will review the file, then sign off on the loan. From under-writing, your loan goes to the lenders' closing department, where closing papers are prepared for you to sign, and where they make certain that everything the underwriter went over is included in your file. For example, if the underwriter asked for an updated insurance policy, the closer would make sure the new policy is included with the loan file.

You arrive at your closing, sign your closing papers, and re-turn home. The person who handled your closing will make sure your loan is closed, with regard to lender requirements and state law. Then he'll send the file back again to the lender. The lender will once again review the file for compliance.

Next, the loan is *funded*—money is electronically withdrawn from the lender's bank account and used to pay off the old lender. In the process, you will receive any money you asked for, if this is a cash-out loan.

Refinance Loans and Escrow/Impound Accounts

Many loans have *escrow accounts* (sometimes known as *impound accounts*) with their mortgage payment. Escrow accounts are funds the borrower saves up to pay property taxes, homeowner's insurance, and *homeowner's association dues*, or *HOA* payments. In addition to the principal and interest, borrowers elect to pay a portion of their annual tax bill and a portion of their insurance premium. Then, as taxes or insurance premiums become due, the lender—who has been collecting these monthly payments —disburses the funds on behalf of the borrower.

A house payment is made up of *principal and interest,* or *P&I.* When you add *taxes and insurance* to that, you get *PITI.* But there's a twist when refinancing a note that has escrow accounts: lenders can't transfer an escrow account to a new lender. That means when you refinance a mortgage with escrow accounts, you must establish a brand new escrow account with the new lender.

Let's say your PITI payment is $2,000 and your principal and interest payment is $1,500, your tax escrow payment is $400, and your insurance payment is $100. If your taxes and insurance both renew on January 1 of each year, then after 2 months, your tax escrow balance is $800 and your insurance account balance is $200. If you refinanced a mortgage that has escrow accounts with $800 and $200 in the respective accounts, then when you refinance the old mortgage into a new one, you'll have to make up the $800 and $200 out of your own pocket, either by providing a check for them at closing, rolling them into your new loan, or some combination thereof.

What happens to your $800 and $200? The old lender will send those funds directly to you within 5–10 business days. You'll get a check in the mail for $1,000. It's up to you to decide how to pay for the new account, but the younger the account, the easier it is to dip into your own bank account for the $1,000, and then replace those funds when you receive your escrow refund.

But what if it's much later in your tax and insurance year? If you have to replace your 10-month-old escrow accounts, you'd have to bring $4,000 for taxes and $1,000 for insurance to your closing. Or not. One way to handle this situation toward the end of the tax and insurance year is to elect *not* to have escrow accounts on your newly refinanced loan. You simply establish them later, after the loan closes and taxes and insurance have been paid. This accomplishes two things: if it's 10 months into the tax year, it's likely that your property tax bills are due and your insurance coverage is coming up for renewal. By choosing not to escrow for taxes and insurance on your new loan, you'll have the funds to pay both of those obligations in about 5–10 business days.

After you pay your taxes and insurance, contact your lender and tell them you'd like to establish another escrow account. And you'll do so at the new tax year, with just one month's taxes and one month's insurance, just as you've always done.

◆ CHAPTER THREE ◆

Finding the Best Lender

This could appear to be either an easy process or a daunting one. It seems mortgage companies are everywhere—at your bank or credit union, on the Internet, even on yard signs placed along the side of the road.

Yes, lenders are everywhere. But why? And why haven't you heard of them all? Because not everyone who advertises for mortgages is a lender. Some are mortgage brokers. Still others are correspondent lenders. The smaller the mortgage operation, the less likelihood they have any advertising budget, or perhaps they choose not to market themselves to the public. What gives? Why are there so many different kinds of mortgage companies that do refinance loans? Because there are so many different ways to get a refinance loan to market.

Mortgages: A Commodities Market

Mortgage loans are really a *commodity*, and are actually designed to be so. What is a commodity? Perhaps one of the best definitions is that a commodity is an item whose only determining value is price.

61

If a blue widget is the exact same item at every widget store and is sold only at convenience stores, then the way to determine the best deal is not to look for differences between blue widgets—there are none—but to find who has the lowest price.

It's the very same with a mortgage. Mortgage loans are exactly the same from one lender to the next, but you wouldn't know that from all the advertisements you see. How can mortgage loans be the same from one lender to the next, if all you hear is how great one lender is compared to the competition? Fannie Mae and Freddie Mac made it so.

Fannie's and Freddie's goals are the same: to foster home ownership. They do this by providing liquidity—cash—to the mortgage marketplace. Before Fannie's and Freddie's "liquidity," when a bank wanted to make a mortgage loan it would do so by first determining if the borrower was creditworthy. In fact, in those days before things such as discrimination laws were in place, a bank could approve or decline a mortgage loan applicant for whatever reason it wanted. "He's too old—he'll probably die before the term of the loan is over" or "We don't lend to women" or "We won't lend to a young couple; what if she gets pregnant?" and other seemingly laughable reasons were common. But it was true. When a bank *did* find someone to whom they wanted to lend money, though, the bank would literally open its vaults and give money to the borrower, who would, in turn, give it to the seller of the house.

Now let's take that scenario a bit further. Say it's the 1930s, and a bank with $100,000 in its vaults wants to make home loans at 5 percent interest. They advertise the new loan rate in the newspapers, and soon they have more business than they can handle. Soon enough, the bank has loaned $10,000 each to 10 home buyers. Remember, this is in the 1930s. But because their offer was so attractive, they had more people lining up to borrow money who could also open up new checking and savings accounts. They had customers turned away, not because the people weren't creditworthy (or too old, or female, or young and married) but because they ran out of cash. This slowed home sales and helped keep an otherwise healthy economy in check.

Government Sponsored Enterprises (GSEs) such as Fannie Mae and Freddie Mac were formed to fix this problem, and they made a pledge: "If a bank makes a mortgage loan under specific guidelines that we set ahead of time, we promise to buy mortgages from you and replace them with more cash to lend." What sort of guidelines? There are lots, but in general the guidelines cover things such as:

- Maximum loan amounts

- Maximum debt ratios

- Minimum credit requirements

And so on—other requirements that forbid things such as not making loans to older people, women, young couples and, well, you get the picture.

But a loan is a loan is a loan. And most every lender offers the same product. A 30-year fixed-rate at Lender A will be the very same at Lender B. But you'd hardly know it by all the advertising you see. Since the GSEs provide liquidity by buying and selling mortgages, you can feel comfortable knowing that there really aren't hundreds of lender types offering a multitude of mortgage options. That alone can help with the confusion. Different lender types are nothing more than a different way to get the product (a mortgage) to market (the consumer).

Who's Who in the Mortgage Process?

So, what are all these differences exactly?

Mortgage Banker

A mortgage banker is so-called because it lends its own money. Or perhaps more correctly, it makes a mortgage loan for which it is responsible, typically from a line of credit. A mortgage banker can be your bank or credit union. When you walk into your bank, you've probably noticed that there are different departments, such as student loans, credit cards, automobile loans and—you guessed it—home mortgages. It can even be a *pure play* mortgage banker. Let's explain.

A retail bank doesn't want just your checking and savings accounts, but your mortgage, too, as well as everything about you from a financial perspective, for that matter. A credit union operates similarly, offering a variety of financial services and products. A pure play mortgage banker is a company that does nothing but issue mortgage loans. A banker, in this capacity, doesn't want your checking or savings account business because it's not actually a bank.

A pure play mortgage banker may be a bit more competitive than a bank in terms of interest rates. On the other hand, a retail bank that offers a variety of financial products may have an edge over a mortgage bank in terms of trust and reliability. Consumers may feel more comfortable with their own bank, even if the rate is 0.125 percent or so higher than a mortgage bank. A mortgage bank may or may not keep your loan after your loan has closed. Often, your mortgage loan is sold. A lender may choose to sell your loan to another lender to free up cash to lend, just as it may sell a loan to Fannie Mae or Freddie Mac.

The loans bought and sold are identical; they're underwritten to the very same standards. They are a commodity. A lender knows exactly what he is buying without ever seeing the mortgage loan, and a seller knows exactly what he is selling. Lenders buy and sell loans to free up cash for more lending, or to stop the lending process altogether and simply make money on the interest being collected each month.

A mortgage loan can be sold multiple times. I'm often asked if the lender who is buying the loan can change the loan or somehow call the note in. The answer is, "No." The new lender can do no such thing. If the buying lender could change the terms of a new loan they bought, that loan would no longer be a commodity; it would be modified by the new lender, which is forbidden by Fannie and Freddie guidelines.

The selling and buying of mortgage loans also helps keep overall interest rates down. All day long, each and every business day, mortgage companies are in a constant flux of buying and selling. This keeps interest rates in check. A mortgage banker also has a credit line they use to fund their loans and borrow against those funds on a very short-term basis—sometimes just a few days, while they complete the sale to a willing lender.

Mortgage Broker

Mortgage brokers also provide mortgage refinance loans, but they don't have their own funds. Instead, they find other lenders to supply the cash. Does that make mortgage brokers more expensive than mortgage bankers? If not, how do the brokers make money? Mortgage brokers get mortgages cheaper than the consumer because they do it on a wholesale basis.

There are a variety of ways lenders can get the mortgages in front of the consumer: with a website, at an office, or in a bank branch, for instance. But *wholesale* lenders do it differently. Wholesale mortgage lenders use mortgage brokers to get their mortgage loans out to the public. Why do wholesale lenders do this? Low overhead.

Any bank, credit union, or mortgage banker has an office. They also have employees and everything else associated with running a business, including utility bills, computers, cell phones, and employee benefits. All these costs add up.

Instead of opening a "retail" mortgage operation, wholesale lenders find mortgage brokers to market their mortgages for them. In turn for having the mortgage broker supply the infrastructure to distribute those mortgage loans, the wholesale lender offers mortgage products at reduced prices to the broker. The broker then marks up that wholesale loan to retail. If prevailing interest rates on a 30-year fixed-rate are at 6.50 percent, a mortgage broker can get that same loan at 6.25 percent. After marking up the rate, the broker makes its money.

Wholesale lenders compete with one another on price as well as service to the mortgage broker. If every wholesale lender were offering mortgage loans at 6 percent, and suddenly another lender offered the same loan at 5.75 percent, where do you think mortgage brokers would start sending all their loans? On the other hand, if every wholesale lender were offering 6 percent, and suddenly another wholesale lender offered the same loan at 6.25 percent, do you think the higher wholesale lender would be in business for very long? Unless there's something remarkably special about that 6.25 percent loan, the lender will either have to revise pricing to match their competitors' rates, or shut down.

Brokers don't approve the loan or issue mortgage funds. They simply find mortgage customers for the wholesale mortgage banker. Brokers will take a mortgage application, document the file, and run credit reports, but they don't provide funds. They have access to multiple lenders and multiple rate choices, whereas bankers do not. That is, unless that banker is a correspondent banker.

Correspondent Banker

A *correspondent banker* is a mortgage banker that operates much like a mortgage broker; it also chooses from various mortgage bankers who find other correspondent bankers to market their products. Correspondent bankers do not collect monthly payments on mortgages. They sell each and every loan individually to other mortgage bankers who use correspondent bankers to distribute their mortgage products.

The difference is that a correspondent takes on much more responsibility than a mortgage broker. A correspondent doesn't just take the loan application, document the file, and run credit reports. It also approves the loan under predetermined GSE guidelines, as well as providing initial funds for the loan. The correspondent banker guarantees that the loan meets Fannie Mae and Freddie Mac guidelines, and also warrants VA, FHA, and other government-backed loans. This is no easy task. Not everyone can set up a correspondent banking business. It requires a minimum net worth, loads of experience, and a credit line that can fund—at least temporarily—millions of dollars worth of mortgage loans.

By approving the loan and guaranteeing its compliance, mortgage banks that use correspondent bankers also issue mortgage pricing that is a tad better than what a mortgage broker can get, at least on a day-to-day basis. In the same way that mortgage brokers get rate sheets and mortgage pricing from a multitude of mortgage companies, correspondent bankers get competitive price quotes from other mortgage banks, most often at a slightly better rate.

Banker, Broker, or Correspondent?

So hands-down, the best choice is a mortgage broker, since mortgage brokers can find the best rate?

That depends. Most mortgage brokers, bankers, and correspondent banks have names you've never heard of. Most don't advertise but market exclusively with business relationships established with other professionals such as Realtors, CPAs, or attorneys. If you're a bit leery of working with a mortgage broker who operates out of his house (even if he quoted you a great rate), and you're uncomfortable giving someone you don't know your personal information, then your bank or credit union may be your best choice.

Banks and credit unions won't always have the absolute best rate, but they'll be competitive. In fact, many credit unions can offer still lower rates depending on how they price mortgage loans to their credit union members. You won't find a bank at 8 percent and a mortgage broker at 6 percent, for example (at least not for the same loan). Mortgage brokers will usually have better interest rates than banks. Mortgage banks and correspondent banks may also have more competitive pricing and will be much more competitive with a mortgage broker than a retail bank will be. And mortgage banks have one more thing that gives them an advantage: control.

I first got into this business as a mortgage broker in San Diego, back in 1990. I was immediately fascinated by the business, especially since mortgage brokerage operations were just beginning to make a major impact in the conventional lending market. Each day on my fax machine, I would receive a multitude of rate sheets from different wholesale lenders. I would carefully compare each rate sheet, looking for the one wholesale lender that offered the absolute best, lowest rate. Sometimes, there would be a wholesale mortgage company that was at least 0.125 percent lower than anyone else. I would immediately advertise the lower rates to my Realtor clients. Very soon, however, other mortgage brokers would begin offering the same rate that I was. I came to the conclusion that while rates *may* vary from lender to lender, they seldom do.

Sometimes, a wholesale mortgage lender who wants to drum up business will offer a rate no other lender would want to meet. This occurs in the wholesale lending environment, when a brand-new company wants to get some mortgage business, and fast! Sometimes, a wholesale lender gets what it asks for: lots of business. In fact, it can get too much business—enough to shut down an operation. I've witnessed this business phenomenon more than a few times over the years. It never ceases to amaze me that these wholesale lenders are rarely equipped to handle the new volume.

When a loan application is submitted to a wholesale lender by a broker, it can take 24 hours for the loan to be approved; then maybe another 24–48 hours to get closing papers to the settlement agency where the borrowers sign their closing documents. As more and more applications deluge the new wholesale lender, business slows to a crawl. Instead of taking 24 hours to get a loan approved, it could take 48. Then 72. Then a full week. And the mortgage broker is helpless. After all, the broker doesn't do any of the underwriting or paperwork. It simply delivers a documented loan application.

If you get an incredible rate from a lender you've never heard of and things are taking longer than necessary and you're getting nervous, it's likely that your loan is stuck in "no-man's land," and no amount of frantic phone calling is going to change things. After all, that wholesale lender is probably sitting on hundreds of loan applications, all to be reviewed. You might find that your refinance application takes weeks to get approved and, ultimately, during that time your interest rate could expire, leaving you vulnerable to higher rates. Granted, this rarely happens, but it *does* happen.

Brokers also have less control over the approval process once it's submitted to the wholesale lender. Sometimes if a lender has a question on a file, the lender doesn't call up the applicant and ask, "Hey, have you ever been known as David Reed, Jr.?" or some similar question. If you were working with a mortgage banker and got a call from your loan officer, you would answer the question, and the loan officer would call the underwriter and say, "No, he's never been known as David Reed, Jr."

A broker has to go through more channels of communication, and once the information finally gets passed to the wholesale lender, the loan has to "get back in line" and wait its turn for review. A mortgage banker, though, can take care of the problem in a more timely fashion than a broker. Brokers might be able to get a slightly better rate, but they lose control of the loan file once it's submitted to the wholesale lender. *Maybe* they might be able to get that slightly better rate, but when comparing a broker to a correspondent banker, then that advantage is no longer important, as a correspondent banker can shop at a multitude of lenders, just as a broker does.

How do you find a correspondent mortgage banker? You won't find any who advertise themselves as "correspondent," but they do have a few characteristics that can help you identify one.

First, correspondents are most likely local or regional mortgage bankers. Those with a national mortgage bank are typically branches or chains of big mortgage banks. Most correspondent mortgage banks are locally owned and have their own credit line where they underwrite to Fannie Mae guidelines and sell the loan after it closes.

But wait! Let's throw one more consideration into the ring: bankers can be brokers, but brokers can't be bankers. A mortgage bank may act as a mortgage broker when a particular loan program is only offered by wholesale lenders. In this capacity, a mortgage bank could send a documented loan file to a wholesale lender, just like an individual mortgage broker does—the best of both worlds, so to speak. So, hands-down, a banker that can also act as a mortgage broker is the best choice for your refinance? Maybe.

There are different motivations for choosing a particular lender. Some consumers are motivated by trust, while others are on a quest for the absolute best rate on the planet. Period. But if you're looking for the best rates possible *and* someone you trust, an established correspondent mortgage banker who can also act as a broker may very well be your best choice.

Can you tell by the name of the company if they're a banker or broker? Probably not. But you can go to their website, click on the "About Us" section, and you should be able to find out there.

Or simply call them and ask them, "Are you a mortgage broker or a mortgage banker?"

After you've narrowed your choices down to a few lenders, you'll want to see if they've been flying straight by contacting the Better Business Bureau and also by contacting the state agency that regulates banks, mortgage bankers, and mortgage brokers. Every state in the U.S. has its own regulatory department that oversees bankers and brokers. Make a phone call or visit the agency's website to see if there have been any complaints on some of the lenders you're thinking of using for your refinance.

Finally, if you're looking to refinance, try looking right under your nose—at your current lender. Call the servicing department and tell them you're thinking of refinancing. If your loan hasn't been sold, you might be in line for a *note modification*. If a modification isn't in order, the servicing department will send you to the loan origination department, where you'll speak with inside loan representatives for that company. You will likely encounter two scenarios.

First, your current lender may assume you're such a loyal customer that they don't have to quote the lowest rate on the planet, as they can make it "easier" for you because they have all of your original information. That might be true, but you still must apply for a mortgage all over again with them. And they can't really use any of your old information, other than your name and Social Security number filled out on a loan application. Everything needs to be updated, a new credit report pulled, title insurance issued, new bank statements, new pay stubs . . . well, you get the picture.

Second, you might find a better deal with a lender who is willing to forgo certain closing costs, should you stay with their company and not move the loan somewhere else. For example, you might get certain lender fees for underwriting or processing waived, or they'll pick up the cost of the appraisal if you stay with them. This can add up to some real savings, especially if you can nail down a great rate, too.

Where *Not* to Look for a Mortgage Lender

The Internet, pop-up ads, and postcards in your mailbox, for starters.

There's nothing wrong with advertising. America's economy is helped along due to advertisements by making people aware of new products or services available to them. And there's nothing wrong with the Internet, either. But we're not talking about buying movie tickets online. This is your mortgage!

Perhaps the most recognized online mortgage operation is Lending Tree. Established in 1998, Lending Tree is not a lender, however. It is a *lead generator* for other mortgage companies. Mortgage lenders pay Lending Tree to be one of the lenders who "bid" on people who log onto Lending Tree's website, submit their information, and wait for the phone to ring.

It used to be said that mortgage companies who use Lending Tree to send them referrals actually bid on a mortgage. This implied that various lenders saw the exact same application and then bid against one another for the privilege of placing a mortgage. In reality, there is no bidding. Your information is handed off to other lenders who will contact you and give you a quote on your mortgage.

Lending Tree soon had imitators. Today, there are several companies online that perform similar functions by placing an online ad, having you fill out a form, and then waiting. These sites are nothing more than lead generators for mortgage companies. After you complete the form, a customer service representative from that lender will contact you with a quote.

There is an advantage to having to complete only one application and having four people contact you. However, it's likely that you won't have heard of the companies who contact you. They may not have an office in your town or aren't familiar with local lending laws in your community. And those lenders aren't going to be any more or less competitive than what you can find down the street at your bank, credit union, mortgage banker, or broker.

If everything goes exactly right with your refinance and you close on time and you got a competitive rate, then all's well that ends well, no? But if there is a problem with your mortgage and you need some help, you may find yourself talking to a loan officer in a distant city, perhaps several time zones away.

Another place not to look for a mortgage is on an online *aggregator* site. An aggregator site is where different lenders advertise their interest rates. The most popular site is Bankrate .com.

Go ahead. Log onto Bankrate.com, click on "Refinancing," then the state and city in which you live, and the type of loan you're looking for, say a 15-year fixed-rate mortgage. Be careful when you click, as there are so many other advertisers that it's likely you'll end up on some other website doing the same thing Bankrate is doing, because Bankrate is *also* a lead generator for other mortgage companies. When you finally make it to the page showing all the rates, be prepared because you'll notice two things—rates are all over the place and they're from mortgage companies you've likely never heard of. No real problem there, but sites like Bankrate.com can't really control how low interest rates can be or take care of "bait and switch" lenders.

When Bankrate first started out in the online interest rate advertising business in the 1990s, my company advertised on it, posting our rates each week. At that time, it was a good resource for both the lender and the consumer, but soon thereafter, companies began quoting unheard-of interest rates with little or no control from Bankrate. Lenders would quote a rate but not disclose pertinent terms such as prepayment penalties, minimum loan amounts, or other "special" qualifications that may wreak havoc on the magically low interest rate.

Bankrate is a great information resource, but there's no valid reason to use a lender found on Bankrate or any other aggregator site. In the next chapter, we'll talk in more detail about how to find the best loan officer for your refinance, but for now, keep in mind that loan officers in your neighborhood or town have reputations to maintain. If a loan officer routinely makes mistakes on mortgage loans, she won't be in the mortgage business for very long. Someone who gets leads from a site like Lending Tree and messes up a loan simply goes back to the pile and gets another lead. I'm sure Lending Tree and others like them are legitimate organizations, but there is no compelling reason to do business with them.

Comparing Loan Choices

When I worked at a mortgage brokerage operation, we used up our fair share of fax paper on the myriad wholesale lenders with which we were authorized to do business, not to mention the vast number of loan programs we offered.

As years progressed, so did the number of new loan variations in the marketplace. In fact, it's not uncommon to find 60 or more loan programs from a single lender, all with at least 15 different interest rate combinations. So far, that's 900 possible loan and rate combinations! Combine that with the various interest rate guarantee periods available—usually four per loan—and the choices become overwhelming. But it doesn't have to be that way. There are actually only 2 types of loan choices—fixed and adjustable. The other 898 are variations on one of those choices. If there are only 2 loan types, then why are there so many choices?

Lenders need to differentiate themselves because their products are commodities—the same thing from one mortgage company to the next. So, they come up with subtle differences in loan properties or give the loan its very own name like, "Payment Stretcher" for an interest-only loan, or "Equity Saver" for a shorter-term loan. They also need to come up with variations on the same thing to make it seem as if they have more choices, either for their mortgage broker or for their banking customers.

Fixed-Rate Loan Types

Fixed-rates never change. They're stable, they're predictable, and they come in five-year increments, starting with 10-year loans. Those are:

10-year fixed

15-year fixed

20-year fixed

25-year fixed

30-year fixed

35-year fixed (although I've not seen lenders offer this, I'm sure it's available)

40-year fixed

50-year fixed (rarely offered, typically only in high-cost areas)

There—all done.

Adjustable-Rate Loan Types (ARM)

6-month ARM

1-year ARM

2/6 ARM

3/6 ARM

3/1 ARM

5/1 ARM

5/6 ARM

10/1 ARM

Payment-option ARM

Negative-amortization ARM

ARMs can get people into trouble, primarily because they have so many components. Worse, when the loans are "spiced up" with loan features such as payment options and negative amortization, it's enough to make even a mortgage broker's eyes glaze over.

In the previous chapter, I advised against refinancing into any ARM if the fully indexed rate is higher than current fixed rates. That is true, but I do want to point out some limited circumstances where those choices might be okay. But first we need to understand the two different types of ARMs: *straight ARMs* and *hybrids*. Both ARM types have the same features:

The index
The margin
The rate cap
The lifetime cap

As described earlier, the index is the base rate at which the mortgage rate is based, and the margin is the amount added to the index to get the new mortgage rate. A common index is the 1-year Treasury bill, and a standard margin is 2.75 percent. If the index today were 5 percent and the margin were 2.75 percent, then the new mortgage rate would be 5 percent + 2.75 percent = 7.75 percent. On a 30-year mortgage with a 7.75 percent on $200,000 the monthly payment is $1,432.

A straight ARM will adjust at preset intervals, most commonly every 6 months or 12 months. If your mortgage rate today were 7.75 percent and you had a 1-year ARM, then 1 year from now the process would start all over again; take the then-current

1-year Treasury bill index, say at 5.25 percent, and add the margin—which doesn't change—of 2.75 percent, to get 5.25 percent + 2.75 percent = 8 percent.

Your monthly payment would be based on your then-current mortgage balance after 1 year at 8 percent, amortized over the remaining 29 years, or $199,799, giving you a new monthly payment of $1,467. Your rate went up because the index increased, but you also paid down your mortgage just a tad, bringing your mortgage payment up by $35 each month.

Let's introduce a scenario. What if inflation hit the fan and next year the 1-year Treasury index hit not 5.25 percent, but 10.25 percent? Now add your margin of 2.75 percent, and your new rate is 13 percent. At 13 percent on $199,799, your new payment nearly doubles to $2,210! Most people can't afford that kind of payment increase, and lenders are well aware of that. That's why lenders put in rate caps, both annual and lifetime caps, to protect consumers (and lenders) from such dramatic payment swings. A common annual cap is 2 percent above the previous year's rate, and a common lifetime cap is 6 percent above the initial interest rate.

If the 1-year Treasury bill indeed went to 10.25 percent, you're protected because even though the "real" interest rate should be 13 percent, it can only go to 9.75 percent, or 2 percent above your initial start rate of 7.75 percent. And if rates continued to rise over the term of the loan, even if the 1-year Treasury bill got to 20 percent it wouldn't matter. The lifetime cap would keep the interest rate no higher than 13.75 percent, 6 percent higher than the initial rate, regardless of what rates do in the future. And rates can go down as well as up!

A hybrid is a cross between an ARM and a fixed-rate. It's fashioned from an ARM, not a fixed, but it acts initially as a fixed-rate because it's fixed for the first few years. A 3/1 hybrid is fixed for 3 years and then turns into a straight ARM. A 5/1 hybrid is fixed for 5 years and then turns into an ARM. A 7/1 hybrid is fixed for 7 years, and so on.

Payment Option ARMs

A *payment option* ARM, or *pay option,* is a newer version of an old theme. Under a payment option ARM, you have four choices each month on what you can pay. Not bad. But if you look under the hood, you'll see that there are some potential problems. Each month you can choose to pay:

The initial "contract" rate, which is well below your fully indexed
   rate (common contract or initial rates can be as low as
   1 percent)
The fully indexed rate
A fully indexed, interest-only rate
A fixed rate, amortized over 15 or 30 years

Looks good, but there's a catch: if you don't pay at least the interest-only rate based on a fully indexed ARM, that difference is added back to your principal balance. For instance, say you have a $500,000 mortgage with a contract rate of 2 percent and a fully indexed rate of 7.50 percent. Your contract rate payment would be $1,848, based on a 30-year amortization (payoff) period. The "real" rate at 7.50 percent would be $3,496 each month. Subtract $1,848 from $3,496, and you get $1,648. You don't have to pay the regular payment, but if you only make the contract payment, then $1,648 gets added back to the original $500,000. In this instance, your loan would grow to $501,648.

Enough of that. Soon, your loan balance could grow to 110 percent of its initial balance, or $550,000. When that happens, suddenly you no longer have options and are forced to pay the "regular" rate of 7.50 percent for the remaining term of the loan. If you're comfortable paying $1,848 each month—but not comfortable paying $3,496 each month—then this loan is not for you.

The only time you should ever consider refinancing into this note is if suddenly your income changes from regular income to *seasonal* income. Seasonal income is income that comes from bonuses once or twice per year, from royalties from a book you wrote, or from sporadic income you make flipping houses as a real estate investor. During the lean times, you could elect to pay just the contract rate. And in the boom times, you make up for it.

Be very wary of this loan. It never amortizes. In fact, it "negatively" amortizes.

Negative Amortization

A *negative-amortization loan*, or *neg-am* loan, isn't just a feature of a pay option ARM; it can simply be an ARM that negatively amortizes if you don't make the fully indexed payment. It's like a pay option ARM, but it just doesn't have the fully amortized fixed option.

Neg-am loans came about in the early 1980s, when interest rates were in the high teens, as in 18 and 19 percent. Homebuyers couldn't afford homes, especially in high-cost areas where home prices are much higher than in other parts of the country. Neg-am loans were then invented by lenders to get people into houses with manageable payments. As long as property values increased and the homeowner occasionally paid the fully indexed rate, then negative amortization was never a problem. I see absolutely no reason to refinance into a loan with possible negative amortization. Should you refinance into an ARM at all? I think it could be a reasonable alternative, in limited circumstances.

If ARM rates are lower than fixed rates, and you'd like a little extra breathing room each month, then you might consider it if you won't be owning that property while the payments are still low. For example, you have a $300,000 mortgage at 7 percent on a 30-year note, with a $1,995 monthly payment. You also know that your employer will be transferring you to another city within three years. A 3/1 ARM might be available at a rate much lower than 7 percent, say 4.75 percent. If you refinanced at 4.75 percent, your new payment would drop to $1,564, saving $431 each month in interest. Your recovery period would be almost seven months, assuming $3,000 in closing costs. In other words, you would save more than $12,000 over three years.

Good idea? Yes. But this instance is based on your company transferring you within three years. What if your company changes its mind? What if it gets bought by another company with a different plan for you? Reasonable assumptions can be made when refinancing into an ARM. Just be aware that "life" can happen to you while you're busy making plans.

Refinancing with Subprime Loans

Subprime loans have been around for decades. Sometimes they're a good thing, and sometimes they're *not* a good thing. But they do fill a particular market niche: loans for those who, for whatever reason, have damaged their credit.

There are two types of people with bad credit: those who ran into some bad times and ruined their credit, and those who couldn't care less about paying anyone back. Subprime loans are for those who used to have good credit but damaged it since the original mortgage was placed. Most often, damaged credit comes from either loss of a job or an illness during which one can't work.

Subprime loans evaluate the person's credit and, most important, the *willingness* to repay a debt. When people have damaged their credit during hard times, subprime lenders help them out. They charge higher rates for that loan, but they do help people out when they most need it.

Refinancing with a subprime loan is often an alternative to bankruptcy. Someone can have bills pile up on him because of a medical situation but still want to pay everyone back, instead of discharging all the debts with a bankruptcy filing. He gets well again and goes back to work, but with a pile of bills and collec-

tion agencies ringing his phone all day long. It would take forever to pay everyone back, so he explores a subprime refinance.

Subprime loans carry higher interest rates and also com-
mand a better equity position than conventional or government
loans do. After all, if a lender is willing to place a mortgage with
someone who has damaged credit, then that lender has a right
to ask for a higher interest rate. Rates for subprime loans can be
as high as 5–6 percent above prevailing rates, when compared to
conventional financing. If current market rates for a standard
mortgage are 7 percent, then a subprime mortgage might have
rates as high as 12 or 13 percent.

That seems high at first glance. But if you compare mortgages to any other credit extension such as credit cards or automobile loans, they seem more than fair. For those with excellent
credit, one might get a credit card rate of, say 8 percent. But if
that person's credit gets damaged or there are late payments on
that same credit card, the interest rate could shoot above 30 percent. That's 30 percent!

If a mortgage company ever even thought of charging 30 percent on a mortgage, the government and every consumer group
in the country would draw and quarter them. Still, subprime
rates are higher than market. So, subprime lenders offer other
loan programs with lower rates, adjustable rate mortgages, and
hybrids.

Hybrids offered by subprime lenders are typically the 2/28,
3/27 or 5/1 format. A 2/28 loan is fixed for two years, then turns
into an ARM for the remaining 28 years of a 30-year term; a

3/27 is fixed for three years then turns into an ARM for the remaining 27 years; and a 5/1 hybrid is fixed for five years, then turns into an annual ARM for the remaining 25 years. (I know the 5/1 moniker doesn't match the 2/28 or 3/27, but that's what they're called.)

Subprime hybrids are offered because their rates are lower than a subprime fixed rate of 12 percent, 13 percent, or higher, depending upon the current credit markets. If a 30-year fixed-rate subprime hybrid is at 12 percent, then a subprime hybrid might be around 8 percent. Subprime hybrids can be an answer to a prayer, or they can be a nightmare. Let's look at this scenario:

Account	Balance	Monthly payment
Current mortgage	$150,000	$997 (7 percent, 30-year fixed)
Collection accounts	$ 30,000	Due now, with penalties and interest
Automobile loan	$ 10,000	$622
Closing costs	$ 3,000	

By refinancing into a 2/28 hybrid at 8 percent, the new scenario would look like this:

Account	Balance	Monthly payment
Subprime hybrid mortgage	$193,000	$1,416 (8 percent, 2/28 hybrid)

The subprime refinance loan has paid off the collection accounts, the automobile loan, and rolled in all the closing costs, and the new monthly payment is almost what the original mortgage payment and automobile loan was.

But now, all the negative accounts have been paid off and the borrower can begin to re-establish his credit history with a brand-new start. That's the "answer to a prayer" part.

Here comes the nightmare part.

Conventional 2/28 hybrids typically have initial caps on them that limit how high their rate can go after the first two years have passed—most usually, no more than 2 percent above what it started out as.

A conventional 2/28 hybrid starting at 5 percent would only rise to 7 percent at the first adjustment. Not so with a subprime hybrid. Many subprime hybrids have no caps and higher margins. Common margins on subprime hybrids are 8 percent. That means if a 2/28 hybrid were based on a 1-year Treasury at 6 percent, and the margin were 8 percent, the new rate after two years would soar to 14 percent. On a $193,000 mortgage, the difference between 8 percent and 14 percent is staggering: $1,416 vs. $2,286. That very nearly *doubled*. Could you handle your current mortgage payment if it doubled after 24 months? Few can. And bad things happen all over again if you can't pay your mortgage.

The Subprime Nightmare

The pitch with subprime loan officers when presenting a hybrid is, "Hey, take this lower rate, re-establish your credit, then refinance into a conventional loan at the end of the two years." This of, course, assumes that no more late payments have occurred and credit is being repaired during this period. The theory works if it's practiced. Get the subprime loan, pay off the bad stuff, and re-establish your credit. Do that and you'll be fine. If not, after two years, the borrower can't, in fact, refinance into a conventional mortgage with lower rates.

Often, two years isn't even enough time to correct one's credit, or maybe there were late payments after the new subprime loan was issued. If so, you can expect to refinance once again into a subprime loan to avoid the initial adjustment. Not sure if two years is enough time? Then take a 3/27 hybrid or, better still, a 5/1 loan. Rates will be slightly higher than a 2/28 loan, yet still lower than a fixed-rate. But now you have more time to pay down the mortgage and re-establish credit.

Okay, now let's stretch this example once more and throw in the fact that property values actually declined rather than appreciated during the two years of the 2/28 hybrid. Guess what? You can't refinance if there's no equity. No matter how much your credit has improved, your loan can't be refinanced without equity. It's possible for you to pay your mortgage loan down to 90 percent of the current appraised value, but that can get expensive.

Go into subprime refinances with eyes wide open. If you play your part well and values hang where they are, you'll be fine.

A few additional cautions on subprime refinances are in order, though. Subprime mortgage loans shouldn't cost more than conventional ones do. The rates will be higher for sure, but in terms of origination charges, points, or lender fees, there is no way you should be paying anything more than 2 points, maximum, for a loan, if even that.

Subprime mortgages are no different from conventional ones when it comes to underwriting standards. Subprime loans have their very own secondary mortgage market where loans are bought and sold. That means subprime loans are the same from one subprime lender to the next. They're all underwritten to the very same previously established guidelines. You might find a shady loan officer who makes it appear that because of your credit situation, it will cost you 5 points and $2,000 in fees, but he can get you out of your mess. Don't do it. You're getting taken.

And just as conventional mortgages have no-point, no fee-loans, so do subprime loans. With subprime loans, a no-point, no-fee loan is your ideal choice. (We'll discuss such loans in even more detail in Chapter 6.) No-point, no-fee loans carry a slightly higher interest rate than loans with points and fees, but the difference in monthly payment is marginal. On a $300,000 subprime loan with one point and $3,000 in fees at 8 percent, the monthly payment is $2,201. By increasing the rate to 8.50 percent, you might get a no-point, no-fee mortgage loan with a payment of $2,306. Yes, the payment is higher than the 8 percent note rate, but you saved $6,000. The recovery period for those two rates is $6,000 / $105 = 57 months.

Your goal with a subprime hybrid is to repair the credit during the initial hybrid years, then refinance into a steady, conventional loan. Paying high points and fees harms you even more, so go with higher-rate, no-cost refinance.

CHAPTER FOUR

Finding the Best Loan Officer

M ortgage companies spend millions upon millions marketing themselves. The mortgage industry is hypercompetitive: just a slight change in a rate or a fee can kill a deal for a lender. But no matter how much money is spent, it only takes one lousy loan officer to mess up the deal. And very often, the lender never knows about it.

Loan officers are the front people for the mortgage company. They're the people you'll interact with throughout the loan process. And it's up to you to get the absolute best loan officer you can find.

What Exactly *Is* a Loan Officer, Anyway?

There is no loan officer "school" or "degree." There are no minimum education requirements. Pretty much *anyone* can be a loan officer, as long as he or she meets the state licensing requirements and takes some kind of test or annual certification. It takes a bit of salesmanship, as well as an ability to communicate and translate complex topics into easy-to-understand tidbits. A knack for numbers certainly helps. Good loan officers always look out for their clients' best interest, and not their own pocket-books. But all in all, loan officers are just like any other professionals.

If you've done your homework and found a lender you're considering working with, how do you check out your loan officer? Or better still, how do you find the absolute best loan officer around?

When you bought your house, whom did you use as your loan officer? Did you like him? Did he treat you fairly? Call him, but by all means make sure he's competing for your loan just like he did the first time. If you didn't like the way things were handled the first time around, you can eliminate that person from your list right away. Get referrals from friends, neighbors, and co-workers and ask whom they used the last time they needed a home loan. If you're thinking of refinancing because rates have dropped, you can bet you're not the only one thinking of a refinance.

I have personally closed mortgage loans for nearly an entire company or organization because word got out that I did a good job. Co-workers talk to one another about their experiences, and, if the loan officer did a good job, you can bet you'll hear about it, especially if you ask. You can also get some good dirt. "Man, don't use so-and-so—they completely screwed up my deal," or something similar. Scratch that one off your list, too.

Perhaps one of the best ways to find a good loan officer is to ask a Realtor for a referral. Why a Realtor?

Good loan officers have been in the business for a several years and they rely on repeat business. One lucrative way to make money as a loan officer is to establish a long-term relationship with a Realtor. Realtors buy and sell homes every day, and when someone uses a Realtor to help him find a home, the Realtor wants to know if the buyers have already spoken with a lender and have been pre-approved. If the buyers haven't been pre-approved, then the Realtor will likely require the buyers to get pre-approved before he shows them any houses.

A Realtor will also have a short list of mortgage loan officers they've done business with in the past, typically giving out two or three loan officer names. This isn't to get a referral fee from the loan officer—referral fees are *illegal*. Instead, the Realtor refers people to loan officers who won't screw up the deal and will make the Realtor look good.

In return, loan officers take these referrals from Realtors, give them one of the most competitive deals around, and close their loan on time, every time. The Realtor looks good because she gave the buyers a solid referral, probably to someone they've never heard of before—and the loan officer makes money.

It takes a lot to get on a Realtor's short list, and often, when a spot becomes available, it's because one of the loan officers on the list quit the business, messed up on a recent deal, or treated his clients poorly. Once a loan officer gets on a list, she tries her darndest to stay there. A good Realtor can provide 20–30 new clients per year to a loan officer. Or even more. A Realtor of that stature has high standards, and his reputation is on the line each time he refers someone to a loan officer. To a loan officer, 20–30 deals per year could be as much as $100,000 in additional income. Not all Realtors have a short list of loan officers, but most who have been in the business for any length of time certainly do. This is especially true for "power" Realtors who buy and sell lots of homes year in and year out, regardless of the market.

If you don't know a Realtor you can call, do a little legwork and find a successful Realtor in your area. One of the easiest ways to find successful Realtors is to visit the Realtor's website and see how many listings that Realtor has—the more listings, the better the Realtor. Some Realtors' websites list industry "partners" where they refer their clients. You might find a list of attorneys the Realtor works with, along with loan officers, insurance agents, and others. If you visit several Realtor websites and keep seeing some of the same names pop up, then you know whomever that Realtor listed on his website must be pretty good. Find the top Realtors in your area and find out whom they send business to.

But you should talk with more than one loan officer—two at least, three at best—to start getting your competitive rate quotes.

Seven Questions to Ask Your Loan Officer

The "rubber meets the road" when you interview your potential loan officer and ask a few questions. At this point, you need to get a feel for the loan officer and how she works by asking seven questions that will reveal much more than a fancy business card or website ever could.

I. *What is your rate today for a 30-year fixed conventional mortgage?* The answer should be quick, precise, and comfortable. Loan officers shouldn't have reluctance quoting an interest rate. You don't want to listen to any hemming and hawing. You want them to get to the point.

2. *What are the lender closing costs on this loan?* If you're talking to a mortgage banker, they'll have this number memorized. Usually it's their company that sets the fees, not the loan officer. If you're talking to a mortgage broker, make sure the fees they're quoting include those from the wholesale lender, as well as from the mortgage broker. When using a broker, there will sometimes be two sets of fees: broker and lender fees. If you just ask for lender fees and don't specifically ask for broker fees, they might not quote them to you because, frankly, you didn't ask. If you're not sure whether the lender is a broker or a banker, you need to ask.

3. *What is the APR for this loan?* This question is the setup from the first two questions. By knowing the interest rate, loan amount, and lender closing costs, the *annual percentage rate,* or APR, can be calculated. Most veteran loan officers, and even the good, not-so-veteran loan officers, have been asked this question so many times their heads spin; it should literally fall off the tongue. If you sense some reluctance from the loan officer, or they tell you that the APR is meaningless, this ought to send up a red flag. You need to work with a loan officer who not only can explain APR properly, but can explain when and why that's an important number.

4. *What is the par price for this loan?* The term *par* means a rate quote with no discount points charged to the borrower to obtain the advertised rate. The term is hidden deep in lending lingo, and if you use the word when interviewing your loan officers, it immediately tells them that you've not just fallen from the turnip truck. For some strange reason, you're familiar with obscure lending jargon—so they'd better not mess with you!

5. *How long have you been in the business?* This seems like a fair question, one that should be asked of almost anyone in any profession. But in the mortgage business it takes on an additional meaning. Let's say you set a doctor's appointment to see about that nagging cough. You sign in, take your seat, and suddenly you see some kid of about 18 years old walking in with your medical chart. Are you going to question this kid's experience? Of course you are. But in reality, physicians spend most of their adult life just getting through medical school, so you won't see any 18-year-olds walking around with a stethoscope. There are requirements for being a doctor.

Are there requirements for being a loan officer? There *are* some, but they're certainly not as rigorous as the requirements for being a physician. There is no national licensing or required training for loan officers, and most U.S. states have their own type of licensing for loan officers. The fact is that almost anyone can be a loan officer. So, asking loan officers how long they've been in business makes perfect sense.

When interest rates drop and homeowners are refinancing their mortgage, suddenly there's a surge of new loan officers in the industry. When rates go back up and business slows, those loan officers get out of the business and go back to being what-ever they were before. You want a loan officer who's good enough at his business to make money when rates are high *and* when they're low. Any loan officer can close a loan during a re-finance boom, but an experienced loan officer knows how to make money during all business cycles. If your loan officer hasn't been in the business for very long, say, only a year or two, I'd rank him a little lower than someone with more experience.

6. *Which lenders do you use?* If you ask mortgage brokers this question, you'll get one of two responses—one straightforward and one vague. The straightforward answer is, "I typically use XYZ Bank, ABC Bank, and HIJ Bank, depending on the loan." The vague answer is, "I really don't know yet until I review all of our lenders. You see, we're signed up with over 100 national lenders, and I'd like to find you the best deal possible."

While that second answer sounds terrific, it's not what you want to hear. Your loan officer should be able to tell you who he's doing business with. There may be names you won't recog-nize, but that shouldn't necessarily cause you any concern. There are lenders who do nothing but wholesale lending. But if your loan officer won't tell you who he's working with, he's not being straight with you. Okay, I'll admit that a loan officer may not know *exactly* where he'll send your loan, but he should have a fairly good idea. If he fails to answer your question, you may want to lower his ranking.

7. *How much money will you make on my loan?* Ouch. This issue of how much a broker will make off you has been around for quite some time, and it's still not fully resolved. But ask your

loan officer how much the company will make on your deal. I know that sounds weird, but think about it this way: your loan officer will ask you the very same question—how much money do you make? Right? Mortgage brokers are required to disclose how much they're going to make on your mortgage loan and will provide you with a good-faith estimate, disclosing who charges what. Most will tell you right away that "We charge an origination fee and a processing fee," for instance, and they'll disclose other third-party loan costs, as well.

Loan Officer Compensation

Knowing how loan officers are paid helps you in the rate negotiation process explained in the next chapter. Most loan officers are paid on a straight commission basis, while some earn a salary plus a small commission.

Smaller mortgage broker and banker operations most likely will pay 100 percent commission to their loan officers. There might be a small starting salary for the first few months to get the new loan officer on track, but typically, if a loan officer doesn't close loans, she doesn't get paid. Like a Realtor or any self-employed person—no business, no money.

Most commission splits are 50/50 between the loan officer and her company. If she makes $3,000 on a loan that closes and she splits everything right down the middle with her employer, she will take home $1,500, and her company will make $1,500, too. As a loan officer matures and regularly brings in more business than his co-workers, it's likely he will command a higher commission split. A loan officer who closes 10 or more loans per month is typically bringing in around $35,000 in revenue to the mortgage firm. In return for bringing in that much business, the mortgage company will offer a higher commission split, sometimes as high as 80 percent or more.

In this example, the loan officer would make 80 percent of $35,000, or $28,000 that month. The company would bring in $7,000. Yes, the commission split is higher than the 50/50 split the $3,000-per-month loan officer gets. But the company still makes more money with a top producer. Top-producing loan officers are always heavily recruited by other mortgage companies. One way to lure a top producer is to offer a higher split.

Most loan officers who work on a salary plus commission are employed by retail banks. Banks pay loan officers less because they don't have to go out and drum up business on their own; they wait for it to walk through the front door of the bank every day.

Qualities of a Good Loan Officer

Good communication. Does the loan officer return phone calls and emails? Do you spend a lot of time tracking this guy down? How did he respond to your calls and your questions? How quickly he gets back to you will be an indication of how quickly he'll get back to you after you've already made an application with him. Does the loan officer work nine to five, or did you get some e-mails with a time stamp on them showing that he works late and answered your e-mails from home in the evening? Good loan officers work round the clock, even on weekends. At the very least, they don't limit their time to regular business hours.

Several years ago, I promised myself that I would never, ever get one of those Blackberry devices. I would have no private time. Realtors and clients would have full access to me 24/7. One day, I broke down and bought one. And I can't believe how much time it saves me. I'm now more efficient. And when I send an e-mail to a client, it says at the bottom that I sent it via Blackberry, meaning the client knows that I'm always available.

Smart. Not necessarily an Einstein, but completely understands the mortgage market and what drives it. Those who have a thorough knowledge of mortgage lending will have a better grip on which loan types will best suit your needs. A lot of that comes from experience, and a lot also comes from studying the market. Loan officers who know a lot about the business have closed a lot of loans. There's really only one way to actually understand any business: do it over and over, don't just read about it in a book. Smart loan officers know shortcuts. They can see red flags in a loan application and address them before they become real problems.

A client once called me up because he was getting conflicting advice from various mortgage loan offices about his situation. He was nearing retirement and was going to buy a new, smaller home after he retired. He asked several mortgage brokers about the little nest egg he'd built up, to the tune of $1.3 million. The mortgage companies he talked to told him, correctly, that lenders can only use dividend and interest income if there's a two-year history of it. He had yet to withdraw any money from that $1.3

million fund, so there was no history, and his Social Security income wasn't going to be enough to qualify him for his retirement home. The guy was 68 years old and was about three months away from retirement. Every loan officer he called talked about reduced-documentation loans that required no verification income or no-documentation loans. Both required a higher rate. He didn't want the higher rate; he wanted the best rate he could find, and I didn't blame him. I told him, "Just buy the house *before* you retire. The lender will use all the income you earn now." He wondered why the other loan officers hadn't told him that. I told him that they didn't know any better.

Stay away from loan officers who bill themselves as "refinance specialists" or some such moniker, or with web addresses like "refi-man.com." Why? Loan officers have to stay in business long-term, and when rates go down, it's "gravy time" for some. As rates move down, loan officers may think they're pretty smart bringing in all this new mortgage business. In truth, all that happened was that interest rates moved downward, making it a good idea for a lot of people to refinance their mortgage loans. So, new business starts pouring in. Mortgage companies pop up overnight to handle this new demand. And since the entry requirements for mortgage loan officers are relatively tame, suddenly loan officers are everywhere, all ready to handle this new influx of business. But rates don't stay low forever. When they move back up, refinance activity dries up and these same refinance specialists go back to doing whatever they were doing before they jumped into the mortgage industry.

The most experienced loan officer is the one who has been through all interest-rate cycles and has been successful at her job even when times were lean. Experienced loan officers get their business from Realtors or CPAs. And in addition to refinancing, they finance homes when people need money to buy.

Friendly. Okay, this might be subjective. But really, why work with someone who rubs you the wrong way? You're getting into a relationship, albeit a short one, but you want to be able to speak up, ask questions, and not feel intimidated.

Refinancing requires spinning a lot of plates, and if you and your loan officer don't hit it off, it's possible that the tension will break up the relationship. Generally, you like people you trust; and if you don't like someone, you're not likely to trust them either. That's why during the interview process, you should take note of how pleasant someone is with you. Does he match your personality? Some people are very direct and can work perfectly with others who are just as direct. (That would seem friendly to someone like me, as I'm direct in my communications.) On the other hand, some people aren't direct and like to chat a little or even have long conversations about this and that before they talk about your mortgage.

Get comfortable with your loan officer. You should like her and she should like you. If your loan officer does her job right, you'll be so happy you'll start referring your friends and co-workers to her. You not only have a business relationship, but you're also friends. What could be better?

Changing Loan Officers

Now let's turn the tables. Your loan officer is an idiot. You did what you could do to find the best one, but it's just not clicking.

You don't like each other, and you work differently. Something's got to change.

Someone once said that an employee is at his best when he first turns in his resume. After that, it's a train wreck. If you make a mistake and things go wrong, can you change lenders midstream and go somewhere else? Yes, but there are some things you need to consider when you do:

Rate locks

Appraisals

Documentation

Time

Rate Locks

If you locked in with one lender, the lock doesn't transfer when you decide to move your loan to another lender; it simply expires. You'll need to re-lock with your new lender and essentially repeat the process you went through with your previous lender.

Another issue with rate locks: wholesale lenders will register your loan when a mortgage broker submits that loan to them and won't honor a new submission from another broker for the very same borrower. The other broker got there first. That's important, if one mortgage lender is being extremely aggressive in the marketplace—"buying" the market with low rates, fees, or both. Mortgage brokers work with the same wholesale lenders. No mortgage broker has a super-secret wholesale lender only he knows about.

When you do cancel a loan with one company and move it to another, there's also the possibility that rates could move in the wrong direction during your loan cancellation process. There's not a whole lot to canceling a loan. You simply call or e-mail the loan officer, and then begin working with someone else.

Appraisals

But let's say you've already invested some money with the old lender. Perhaps you paid for a credit report, an appraisal, or an application fee. If you paid an application fee and want to transfer to a new loan officer, that's money down the drain. (And if the new lender is smart, he'll recognize your propensity to take your business elsewhere if someone makes you mad, so he too will ask for an application fee!)

If you paid money for a credit report, you can't get that back either, and you can't transfer the credit report from one lender to the next. You'll need to pay for a new one. But you *may* transfer the appraisal from one lender to another, so you don't have to pay another $350 dollars or so for a new one. But you *will* have to pay the appraiser for a *re-type,* which is nothing more than changing the appraisal to reflect the new lender's name in place of the old lender. A re-type costs about $50.

You'll also have to sign a piece of paper formally requesting cancellation of your loan with the first lender and stating that you want your appraisal transferred to the new lender. But there's a catch: you may have thought you paid for the appraisal when, in fact, you paid for an "application fee." The loan officer probably told you that the application fee covers the cost of the appraisal. But if you decide to transfer your loan, guess what? The application fee is not refundable. Now the appraiser will ask you to pay for the appraisal before he will transfer it to a new lender. That means you'll pay the $50 re-type fee, and then have to pay about $350 for the appraisal. You need to be aware of these charges when you decide to move your loan.

Documentation

When you request an official transfer, the lender can't just send you the whole file back. They are required by law to keep an original loan application and any documents internally generated. That means they keep anything they asked for either from you, your employer, or your bank. You get copies of those originals, but you don't get the originals. One of the many things lenders are responsible for is to keep track of approved, declined, and canceled loans. If you cancel your loan, the loan application must stay at the old lender, along with an official form that explains why the loan didn't close (for example, "borrower couldn't qualify due to credit" or "borrower changed his mind").

You'll also need to complete a brand-new application with the new lender, along with providing any documentation the new lender requires.

Time

If the markets are moving in the wrong direction and you want to transfer your loan, you may not have time to. If you're locked in with one lender and rates have moved up since then, you just may have to grit your teeth and sign your loan papers.

One of the benefits of a refinance—as opposed to a contract loan—is that you're not locked into closing a loan for a preset time frame. When you first bought the property, the contract clearly stated that you must close by a certain date or you could lose your earnest money. You didn't have the luxury of waiting. With a refinance, you can wait to close until the cows come home. But there's a risk: you can wait and wait, only to watch interest rates go back up again.

When your loan officer isn't as sharp as his resume would have you believe, and you want to shop around, you certainly may. But remember, there are expenses and risks involved. Keep in mind that state agencies regulate and license local loan officers— both mortgage bankers and mortgage brokers. If you wind up with a bad loan officer, don't let him off the hook so lightly. Instead of just taking the hit and moving on to a new loan officer, you should report the old loan officer's negligence or suspicious activity. Don't call up the state licensing bureau just because you didn't get along with your loan officer, but do it when you feel as though he's doing something dishonest or possibly illegal.

CHAPTER FIVE

Finding the Best Interest Rate

Finally. So far, we've been preparing you for this chapter by getting you in the position to find the best rate around. After all of that, we get to the good stuff—getting the absolute best mortgage rate available.

When you see rate quotes in the newspaper or on the Internet, does it appear that they're all over the place? One rate is at 6 percent, while another is at 5.50 percent, while still another is at 5.25 percent with 1 discount point and origination charges. How can everyone have so many different rates? They can't, but they can have variations on the same theme. Let's dig in a little deeper on this.

Small Changes, Big Changes

Mortgage rates are a dynamic lot. They change constantly and throughout the day. Much of these changes are imperceptible, but they do exist. In fact, rates can change by 1/100 of a percent on a moment's notice, or even 5/100 of a percent—up or down. This 1/100 of a percent is called one *basis point*; 2/100 of a percent is 2 basis points, and so on. Small changes, but changes nonetheless.

When these rates approach changes of 50 basis points, then they begin to affect the mortgage rates themselves. A 50-basis-point move will raise or lower a 30-year fixed-rate mortgage by about 1/8 percent, or from 7 percent to 7 1/8 percent. A 100-basis-point move will change the rate by 1/4 percent, or from 7 percent to 7.25 percent.

But doesn't the Federal Reserve Board (or "the Fed") change interest rates? Yes, but not your mortgage rate. I know that sounds a little odd, since many media reports would have you believe that the Fed's actions have a direct effect on your mortgage rate. But that is simply not the case. Unless your rate is based on the prime rate, your mortgage rate is influenced by other factors. The Fed has a general impact, but not a direct one.

How is that so?

One of the main things the Fed controls, or attempts to control, is inflation. And one way to do that is to increase or decrease the cost of money. The cost of money they directly affect is the *Federal Funds Rate,* or *Fed Funds.* The Fed Funds rate is the official government rate that banks charge one another for very, very short-term (overnight) loans. Banks sometimes have to borrow from one another to meet certain daily obligations, such as maintaining a certain level of cash reserves as a percent of outstanding loans. After a bank makes a number of loans, pays out interest, or otherwise depletes its cash position on a given day, it's required to have enough cash available to cover every one of its customers, if they all suddenly decided to close their checking and savings accounts. Think "bank run," and you'll get the picture.

Growing businesses are increasingly starved for more capital so that they can make more money. As the demand for capital increases, so, typically, does the cost of money go up. If more and more businesses want to get their hands on the same wad of cash, banks know they can charge just a little more in interest than when times were slow, so they raise the cost of the money they lend.

When banks increase the cost of money, the businesses don't just roll over. To offset the higher cost of money, they charge higher prices for their products and services. When economies are strong, more people are at work, and when businesses expand, they need more people—sometimes the *same* people. That means businesses must pay their employees more, or lose them to their competitors. Soon, most everything begins to cost more because the cost of money is gradually increasing due to the demand for capital. As demand begins to encroach on supply, inflation begins to rear its ugly head.

Why Inflation Kills Economies

At a 10 percent annual inflation rate, a $10 bill today will be worth $9 one year from today, and less and less each year. Goods cost more not only because demand is higher but because inflation eats away at the future value of things. Businesses must then increase the price of their goods or services to cover this devaluation, but that only feeds the monster, and it starts all over again. Once inflation starts, it's hard to control.

One of the Fed's main goals is to keep inflation in check. They do so by adjusting short-term interest rates. To slow down an overheated economy, the Fed will increase rates, making it more expensive to borrow money. In a slow economy, the Fed will decrease rates. This stimulates the economy by providing cheaper money that will ultimately enable businesses to expand.

The Federal Reserve Board is constantly on the lookout for signs of inflation and at the ready to make adjustments to the cost of money when they meet every six weeks. But keep in mind that when the media report that the Fed "dropped" interest rates by half a percent, it doesn't mean your lender will drop its 30-year fixed-rate mortgage from 7 percent to 6.50 percent. It doesn't work that way.

The Fed does actually have an indirect impact on your mortgage rate. It's based on the prospect of inflation, but from another angle: mortgage bonds.

A mortgage rate is directly tied to its respective mortgage bond. A run-of-the-mill Fannie Mae 30-year fixed-rate mortgage is tied to the Fannie Mae mortgage bond (also known as a *coupon*) currently being traded—literally a 6 percent Fannie Mae 30-year coupon. This is why mortgage rates can't be at 6 percent at one lender and 7 percent at another lender for the very same loan product. All lenders price their 30-year Fannie Mae loan on the very same index. And they watch that index like a hawk—all day, every day.

Mortgage bonds are afraid of inflation because their value is based on current versus future value—just like the $10 bill. Bonds have set returns. It's a guaranteed payout at the end of the term.

Let's say a note seller has some $1,000 bonds that pay 5 percent in interest over a preset term. At the same time, the Dow Jones Industrial Average has been taking a beating, and some investors are getting a little weary of losing money by the bucket. So, instead of investing in stocks, they look at these $1,000 notes. Sure, they only pay 5 percent, but that's a lot better than losing 20 percent, right?

These investors begin buying the bonds at $1,000 a clip. Because of the increase in demand, the seller soon begins raising the price of that bond, and those same $1,000 bonds now cost $1,100 for the same 5 percent return. Sure, the 5 percent is still nice, but it costs a little more now, doesn't it? Because of that rise in price, the *effective* interest rate then drops from 5 percent to 4.55 percent. That's how mortgage bonds work as well. When the price paid for those bonds increases, the rates fall. Inflation eats at the future value of that $1,000 bond, and it will eventually be worth less than it is today. Rates then have to go up to cover the same yield.

Each business day, all day long, various mortgage bonds are bought and sold in markets, along with other commodities and stocks. In a growing economy, investors tend to load up on stocks, while keeping a minimum amount in bonds for safety reasons. In a weaker economy or a tanking stock market, investors pull money out of the riskier stock market and into the safety net of bonds—all types of bonds, including mortgage bonds. If you understand this premise, then you probably know at least as much about how rates are set than most loan officers do. This gives you an idea of the financial competence of your potential loan officer. If your loan officer doesn't understand how rates move each day, then how can he advise you about interest rate trends?

The fact is that he can't. And you might just want to include the question, "How are mortgage rates set each day?" to your list of things to ask.

If you have a loan officer who can easily explain the above, then you've got someone who knows what he's doing. If someone stammers and says things like, "The Fed this" or "The Fed that," then you don't have the most competent loan officer on the planet—or even on the block.

Mortgage Rates and Economic Factors

So why do investors watch what the Fed does or doesn't do? Or more specifically, why do investors watch the economy so closely? They're looking for signs of inflation. The faster the economy is moving along, the greater the likelihood of inflation.

Nearly every business day, various economic reports are released. Each new report show how the economy has been doing over the previous month or quarter. As these reports are released, both the stock market and bond market will react in one fashion or another. A rosy economic report could point to higher rates, while a dour one could signal a slowing economy. Yet, a single report will not affect interest rates, and it won't happen overnight. Instead, a series of reports over a protracted period will make a difference in rates.

When evaluating an economy, economists look at the big picture, not on discrete bits of evidence. If, for instance, in one month's time, the unemployment rate moves from 5 percent to 5.10 percent, investors will wait another month to see if the rate goes back down, stays the same, or increases. If the unemployment rate goes from 5.10 percent to 5.25 percent the following month, and then to 5.50 percent, there's definitely a trend. When more and more people are losing their jobs, it's a sign of a weakening economy, and an indication of lower rates ahead. A slowing economy will move investments out of the stock market and into bonds, including mortgage bonds. As the price of these bonds goes up, mortgage rates will go down.

You need to be aware of economic trends if you're looking at refinancing down the road, and you also need to be aware of the various reports that can impact daily interest rates. This is especially true if you're already in the middle of a refinance application and you haven't "locked in" your interest rate, but are trying to time the market to get the best rate in your situation. It might only be 1/8 percent or so of a change, but that's how mortgage markets move.

It also gives you a critical upper hand when negotiating interest rates with your loan officer. You might ask, "I saw today where the non-farm payroll numbers were way down again last month. We should be seeing lower rates today, right?" When you're following the markets that closely, how can a loan officer pull the wool over your eyes?

How do you identify which reports you should pay attention to? There are a multitude of economic reports, but these are the ones considered most important, with regard to interest rates:

Average Work Week: The number of hours worked each week by all employees. The more hours worked indicates a brisk economy, bringing higher rates.

Construction Spending: More spending means more jobs, a recovering economy, and the possibility for higher rates.

Consumer Confidence: A confident consumer buys more and acquires more debt, which creates higher prices and higher rates.

Consumer Price Index (CPI): An inflation indicator. Higher inflation means higher rates.

Durable Goods Orders: More goods sold means more jobs, a strong economy, higher rates.

Employment Cost Index: The total cost to employers of having employees, including things like payroll and employee benefits. Higher employment costs portend higher costs to consumers and higher rates.

Existing Home Sales: More homes sold means more jobs and a better economy, which can lead to higher rates.

Factory Orders: More orders mean higher rates.

Federal Open Market Committee (FOMC) Meeting: "The Fed" meets eight times per year to evaluate the economy and discuss monetary policy. At these meetings, the Fed Funds rate can be adjusted.

Gross Domestic Product (GDP): More goods produced means a strong economy, which leads to higher rates.

Institute for Supply Management (ISM), formerly called the **Purchasing Managers Index:** More goods sold means a good economy and higher rates.

Leading Economic Indicators (LEI): Forecasts future economic growth. High indicators mean higher rates.

Producer Price Index (PPI): Wholesale inflation numbers. Higher prices for goods mean higher rates.

Retail Sales: Strong retail sales figures mean a strong economy and higher rates.

Unemployment Numbers: Low unemployment and lots of new jobs being created mean higher rates.

Notice that every single report indicated the possibility of higher rates. In reality, the reverse is also true. High unemployment, few jobs being created, or slow retail sales can indicate lower rates ahead. Or the numbers released can be benign. Before each report is released, there is always a "consensus forecast" which estimates what the upcoming report will be. If the consensus forecast for the unemployment rate is 6 percent and the real number released at a later date is, in fact, 6 percent, there will be little movement in interest rates that day, as the markets had already "priced in" that 6 percent figure. Rates will typically only move if reports are above or below economists' forecasts.

Do you need to pore over all these reports each and every day, losing sleep over the retail sales number to be released later this week? No, but you do need to pay attention to the overall picture.

Let's now take the next step: how does your lender set interest rates, if the Fed doesn't set them?

Mortgage lenders have special departments, or *secondary departments,* which price mortgages, set rates, and buy and sell mortgage loans. Secondary departments have teams of people who keep their eyes glued to the mortgage bond market in case of wild swings. Each morning at about 10:00 a.m. (EST), many of the economic reports will have been released, and bond traders react. Secondary departments watch the price of their particular mortgage bond and set their rates accordingly.

If a 30-year mortgage bond closed yesterday at a price of 100 basis points and opened the next day at 100, then lenders would issue their mortgage rates at the same rate as the previous day, because the price of that mortgage bond didn't move. But say later on that day, an economic report is released indicating the economy is still in a decline. Investors will start pulling money out of the stock market and putting it into the safe haven of bonds, including mortgage bonds.

Suddenly, the price of that mortgage bond shoots from 100 to 100.50, a 50-basis-point move. By mid-day, in an effort to keep competitive in the mortgage market, lenders re-price their mort-gages and reduce them by 1/8 percent. Later on that day, another report shows that the economy is slowing even more, and the stock market begins to take a nosedive, driving up the price of bonds. Bonds now rise another 50 basis points to 101, and lend-ers make another change by decreasing rates another 1/8 per-cent.

In one day, interest rates dropped by 1/4 percent!

The previous example is rare, but rates *will* move throughout the day. Most days, a mortgage bond will move just a few basis points as bonds are bought and sold. A bond may move from 100.26 to 100.34, for example. That's not enough for lenders to re-price their mortgage rates.

After a couple of weeks or so of gradual price increases, lend-ers will change their rates as bond prices dictate. Lenders can't issue a mortgage rate of 7.125687 percent. Well, they could, but lenders limit rate changes in 1/8 percent increments. I've seen markets change by 1/4 percent or more perhaps just a few times in my 20-year career in the mortgage business. It just doesn't happen that often. Markets typically aren't surprised by eco-nomic data.

Let's throw in another item that can move markets: political events. Besides economic news, *political* news can also roil the interest-rate markets. There's no reason to list a number of polit-ical events that can make rates go higher or lower but, in general, be aware of anything happening that could possibly bring about such things as wars, assassinations, a disruption of oil supplies—these things can all impact mortgage rates. During uncertain geopolitical times, money will move out of stock markets and into safe havens such as bonds or gold. You can watch economic report after economic report showing a rosy economy with home sales rising, unemployment rates dropping, and more people at work. And then, out of nowhere, one far-off political event can rattle everything, if the impact is great enough.

Lenders set their interest rates each day using the corresponding mortgage bond as their index. But it's important to note that lenders won't issue just one rate. They'll issue a "spread" of interest rates based on that same index.

A *discount point* is 100 basis points, or 1 percent of the loan amount. A point is used to "buy down" an interest rate from one point to another. For instance, if your loan officer is quoting you 7 percent with zero points, you can buy down that interest rate from 7 percent to 6.75 percent by paying 1 discount point. On a $300,000 loan, then, 1 point equals 1 percent of $300,000, or $3,000. If you wanted to pay 2 points, your rate would typically be reduced yet again from 6.75 percent to 6.50 percent throughout the life of the loan. A lender will take that $6,000 up front, in lieu of collecting interest at the higher rate of 7 percent over an extended period. Discount points are a form of prepaid mortgage interest and are tax deductible, just as mortgage interest is.

When lenders set rates, they will issue a variety of mortgage rates to their loan officers which will look something like the following.

For a 30-year fixed-rate:

Rate	15-Day	30-Day
7.625%	(4.087)	(3.962)
7.50%	(3.798)	(3.673)
7.375%	(4.000)	(3.875)
7.25%	(3.828)	(3.703)
7.125%	(3.423)	(3.298)
7%	(3.203)	(3.078)
6.875%	(2.944)	(2.819)
6.75%	(2.668)	(2.543)
6.625%	(2.308)	(2.183)
6.50%	(1.920)	(1.795)
6.375%	(1.412)	(1.287)
6.25%	(0.997)	(0.872)
6.125%	(0.522)	(0.397)
6%	(0.006)	0.119

For a 20-year fixed-rate:

Rate	15-Day	30-Day
7%	(3.147)	(3.022)
6.875%	(2.608)	(2.483)
6.75%	(2.425)	(2.300)
6.625%	(2.159)	(2.034)
6.50%	(1.865)	(1.740)
6.375%	(1.463)	(1.338)
6.25%	(0.949)	(0.824)
6.125%	(0.382)	(0.257)
6%	0.0440	.169
5.875%	0.530	0.655
5.75%	1.198	1.323

5.625%	1.929	2.054
5.50%	2.433	2.558

For a 15-year fixed-rate:

Rate	15-Day	30-Day
6.625%	(3.094)	(2.969)
6.50%	(2.748)	(2.623)
6.375%	(2.530)	(2.405)
6.25%	(2.143)	(2.018)
6.125%	(1.780)	(1.655)
6%	(1.393)	(1.268)
5.875%	(1.093)	(0.968)
5.75%	(0.605)	(0.480)
5.625%	(0.218)	(0.093)
5.50%	0.170	0.295
5.375%	0.495	0.620
5.25%	0.932	1.057
5.125%	1.370	1.495
5%	1.807	1.932

These are not the rates you'll get, as the loan officer has yet to mark them up to retail level. But you'll notice that the lower the rate is, the more points you'll pay. You'll also see that a 50-basis-point change in price is not universal, but a *general* guideline. For instance, on a 15-year rate at 5.50 percent and 15 days, the "wholesale" cost is 0.170 points. On $300,000, that results in $510. If the loan officer wanted to make a total of 1 point off of you, he would add the 0.170 to 1 discount point, and the result would be 5.50 percent, and 1.17 points to you. Most often, however, the loan officer would simply quote you 1 point or 1.25 points, and not the .17.

The 15- and 30-day columns indicate how long that rate will be good—the "lock in" term. The longer you need a rate guaranteed, the more it will cost you.

You'll also notice the brackets around some of the prices. This indicates a "negative" number. The higher the rate, the higher the negative number, or *Yield Spread Premium*, that mortgage brokers receive. Yield Spread Premium, or YSP, has gotten a bad name because of some abusive lending practices, but, in general the higher the rate, the greater the YSP. On at 15-year fixed-rate at 6.625 percent, the YSP is (3.094) for 15 days. On a $300,000 mortgage that yields $9,282, that goes from the lender to the loan officer as income. And that's a lot. Typically, however, a loan officer will make between 1 and 2 points total on a deal, and the YSP gives the consumer the option of paying points or paying no points at all.

If you decided to pay no points on a mortgage, then how does the loan officer get paid? From the YSP. Again, in the 15-year fixed-rate chart, with the loan officer making about 1 point, he would quote you either 5.875 percent or 6 percent. You elected to take a higher rate in lieu of paying points. We'll discuss points and closing costs in more detail in the next chapter.

Rate Shopping

Playing the "rate game" can get a bit dicey. Getting interest-rate quotes can feel like a shell game, with loan officers quoting one interest rate for one time period with so many points, another rate for a shorter time period with fewer points, and so on. The first thing you must do is decide beforehand the exact type of loan program you want. Then, don't budge from that decision.

Mortgage rates can't be all that different from one lender to another, and a variance of only 1/8 percent is common from one lender to the next. But let's say that you did identify which lenders you'd like to get quotes from and determine that a 20-year fixed-rate mortgage is perfect for you.

Lender A is quoting you 6 percent, and Lender B is quoting you 6.125 percent. You decide to go with Lender A because the rate is better, but Lender B, who knows that he's lost your business, calls you and says something like, "You know, I have a special deal today on a 15-year fixed and I could also arrange to pay for your appraisal. I can get you 5.875 percent on a 15-year fixed and waive your appraisal charges, but I need you to lock in with me right now," or some such pitch.

It could even be, "Say, I noticed you've got a couple of kids in high school and thought you could refinance and pull money out for college at the same time. If you change from a 20-year fixed-rate loan program to my 7/1 hybrid ARM, you could lower your payments while pulling out an additional $15,000. I'd also be willing to pay for some of your closing costs as well. How does that sound?" Yes, you've got kids going to college soon and no, you don't have a wad of cash sitting in a college fund somewhere, so you run the numbers and, sure enough, you'd have lower payments and $15,000. So you call the loan officer back and say, "Sure, let's do it!"

You just lost the rate-shopping game.

When loan officers aren't competitive on a particular day for a particular product, they'll try and switch you into something they're more competitive on—in this instance, a cash-out 7/1 hybrid. If you do want to change your loan program, you'll need to start all over and call the other lenders to quote on the new program.

It's also possible that you haven't decided which loan program to take and would like some input from a professional loan officer. It's free. Just call up one of the loan officers you're thinking of doing business with and tell him your scenario:

"I'm just thinking of lowering my rate."

"I'm just thinking of lowering my rate and maybe pulling some cash out."

"I'm just thinking of lowering my payments to as low as they can be, for three to five years."

"I'm just thinking of lowering my rate and reducing my loan term."

Lenders can be creative when it comes to presenting you with various loans, and seasoned loan officers know how to design a mortgage around your current situation and your particular requirements. If you don't know which loan you want, but you think that a refinance is in your best interest, call and get some counseling before shopping around for the best rate.

When to Call

The time to start shopping around for interest rates is around 11:00 a.m. (EST). When the bond markets open up in the morning, there will likely be very little trading until certain economic reports are released and the stock and bond markets have had time to digest the data. At the same time, lenders will typically "shut off" rate quotes at the end of their business day. If you got a rate quote from yesterday at 6 percent and call *today,* you won't get yesterdays' quotes—you'll get the current rates. Once the markets have had time to settle in, the lender's secondary mortgage department will compile its interest rates and distribute them to their loan officers or mortgage brokers, so there's no use in calling anyone for a rate quote until midmorning because rates have yet to be released at that point.

Another critical piece to this puzzle is making sure you place your mortgage rate calls as closely together as possible. If you got a rate quote from Lender A at 11:00 a.m. and didn't call Lender B until 4:00 p.m. that same day, it's not fair to either Lender, as rates could have moved during the day. When markets become volatile, lenders will start to reprice their loans, usually when bond prices go higher or lower by about 16 basis points.

Lenders won't go through all the effort needed to re-price more than 30 different loan programs, all with different rates attached, unless there's a big enough swing in one direction or the other, and 16 basis points is normally the tipping point. If Lender A quotes you 6 percent and Lender B quotes you 5.75 percent, then it's possible the markets changed for the better during the business day, not that you didn't find the lowest lender on the planet. If, in fact, Lender B quotes you 5.75 percent, then you'd better make a quick call to Lender A to double-check their rate quote.

It's also necessary to get a rate quote for the period needed to close your loan. If you're shopping for rates and haven't applied anywhere, then you probably need 30 days at most to close your loan. That's how long you need to get your rate quoted for.

Sometimes, a loan officer can "lowball" an interest rate that she, in fact, might have available on her rate sheet for only a very, very short period of time, say 5–10 calendar days. That's not enough time to complete your refinance transaction. If you simply call some loan officer up and ask him, "What's your 30-year fixed-rate today?" do you think they'll quote you interest rates that are good for three to four months? Of course not. They'll likely quote you the rates for their shortest term. It makes them appear to have lower rates than their competitors. When you call and get rate quotes, you have to specify for how long you need the quote for. Always use the 30-day lock period as your guideline because everyone offers that period.

Keep in mind that rate quotes assume you have good credit. Just because a lender quotes you 6 percent, it doesn't mean you'll get it if your credit has been damaged. Rate quotes also assume you have a minimum equity position in your house and that you occupy the property you're refinancing. If you're not, the rate will be a little higher.

Loan officers can also jumble up the rate quote by giving you various interest rate point and rate combinations. You may call up a lender and get:

Rate	30-Day
6%	0 pts
5.875%	½ pt
5.75%	1 pt
5.625%	1¼ pt
5.50%	2 pts

Then, you might call another lender and get:

Rate	30-Day
6%	0 pts
5.875%	½ pt
5.75%	1¼ pt
5.625%	1½ pt
5.50%	1¾ pt

Confusing? It *can* be. Rate shopping is hard enough without comparing different rates from the same lender for the very same loan program. It's easy to think that lenders do this on purpose, to make the process bewildering. And while that might appear to be the case, it's really not. Or at least it's not *supposed* to be that way. It's simply that mortgage bonds, pricing, and the markets make for a confusing animal, in the first place.

The way to clear the air is to decide not only on the loan program you want and how long you want the quote for, but also how many (if any) points you want to pay. Instead of asking for 30-year rate quotes, say, "Give me your 30-day quote on a 20-year mortgage, if I pay 1 point and if I pay zero points." In this way, you'll truly be comparing apples to apples. You'll now get the perfect rate quote. But you're not done.

It's likely that you have two similar rate quotes, and the loan officers you've been working with have spent some time on their end preparing quotes, following up on e-mails, and exchanging voice mails with you. Now call both of them and say, "Your rate looks pretty good, and I will lock today with you if you can come down another 1/8 point." A difference of 1/8 of a point is not much. It won't drop your mortgage rate at all. But at this stage, it starts to eat away at the loan officer's commission. When you ask for 1/8, you're not asking for a lower rate, but slightly less in charges to you.

When you ask that question, the loan officer immediately begins to consider it by thinking: *Okay, 1/8 point on $300,000 is $375. Since I would split that with my company, I'm really only giving up $187.50. After taxes, that's really only $130 or so.* "I'll accept your offer!" says the loan officer.

Since you made the commitment, you need to follow through with your lock. After you hang up, call the other loan officer and make the same offer. But what if the rates are exactly the same and you've gotten the very same quote from both of your potential loan officers? Then it's splitting hairs at this stage—if you've received some very competitive rate quotes, then it's nothing more than working with someone you liked better or someone who returned your calls and e-mails more quickly.

Rate Locks

Now that you've got the rate you want, what do you do with it? First, get it guaranteed, or *locked in*. Just because you've been quoted a rate over the phone doesn't mean it's yours. You must request a rate lock before you can claim it.

There are no universal lock procedures. One lender's lock policy will differ from another's. But when you lock in, there are a few requirements that you can always expect. Most lenders won't lock you in unless they've seen your loan application and credit report. This means you'll have to make a formal loan application, which can usually be completed online. Some lenders ask that you pay for an appraisal up front. Some charge an application fee (which, in essence, goes to pay for your appraisal), while others make no such requests.

One thing you don't want to do is wait to complete a loan application while you keep your eye on interest rates. You could get a rate quote in the morning and submit a loan application later that day, only to discover that the rates moved before your application was reviewed. So, if you're serious about a lender and you get a quote for a rate you want, it makes sense to put in a loan application with that lender. (It also helps your negotiation process when the loan officer sees that you're serious enough about refinancing to have taken the time to fill out their loan application.)

Once your application is approved and reviewed, when the interest rate hits your target rate you simply call up the loan officer, say, "Lock me in," and away you go! When you do get your rate locked in, it's crucial to get the agreement in writing. If you get your rate quoted to you verbally be sure and ask for that written lock agreement. Note, too, that if you're working with a mortgage broker, you're really not locking in with the broker. You're asking the broker to lock you in with one of their lenders. When a broker requests a rate lock for one of their borrowers, it takes a bit more time. The broker either has to log onto the lender's website, upload your loan to them, or request a specific lock.

Locks from lenders aren't any good until that broker receives a confirmation of your lock request. The broker will then take that information and issue their lock confirmation to you. The lock confirmation should contain:

The interest rate you requested

Any points that rate cost you (if any)

Length of lock period

Loan amount

While your rate is locked, your loan is being processed by having an appraisal ordered or by gathering insurance information or pay stubs from you. The lock doesn't guarantee you a loan approval. If the value of the property doesn't come in as expected or some negative credit items suddenly appear, the lender is not obligated to issue you a refinance. The only guarantee is that *if* your loan closes, it will close at the rate you requested. If you don't get your lock confirmation within 24 hours of requesting your lock, call your loan officer and ask, "Hey, what gives?" From time to time, a loan officer may simply "forget" to lock you in (sometimes, he forgets on purpose). Your phone call or e-mail will jog his memory.

Market Gains

Loan officers follow mortgage rates on a daily basis. Some even subscribe to special mortgage-bond services that alert a loan officer when mortgage bonds are trading up or down by, say, 16

A sample lock confirm/lock float agreement.

A LETHES LLC PRICING POLICY

Application Date _____

Loan Originator _____

Application Name(s) _____

Listing Agent _____

_____

Selling Agent _____

Property Address _____

(**X**)   **Float Option:** Loan applications may "float" until the applicant(s) chooses to lock a specific interest rate and discount points (together known as "price"). Because Alethes LLC reserves the right to change the prices it offers more than once each day, it is important that an Alethes LLC representative is contacted immediately once a decision to lock-in is made by the applicant(s). Furthermore, the Alethes LLC representative must confirm all prices with Alethes LLC's marketing department or chosen investor prior to confirmation of a lock-in.

( )   **Lock-In Option:** The interest rate and discount points are guaranteed for a specified number of days, per the term of the LOCK-IN AGREEMENT contained below. Upon notification from the applicant(s), or the listing or selling agent, of an intent to lock a rate and points, Alethes LLC will guarantee the lock-in price despite any subsequent market rate changes, either up or down, until the lock-in expiration date, as provided in a completed LOCK-IN AGREEMENT signed by the applicant(s). Refinance loans are eligible only for _____ day lock-in. Alethes LLC's policy on expired lock-ins is as follows: The LOCK-IN AGREEMENT establishes the <u>minimum</u> price that Alethes LLC will guarantee to the applicant(s) for a loan. If the lock-in expires, the loan will close at the expired lock-in price or the prevailing market price, **whichever is greater.** Under no condition can the loan close at less than the original lock-in price.

I/We have applied to Alethes LLC for a home mortgage loan. By my/our execution hereof, I/we acknowledge and understand that fees paid for credit reports and appraisals are for expenses incurred to third parties in the process of obtaining this loan and are not refundable; and that any guarantees by Alethes LLC of an interest rate and/or discount points to me/us will expire if this loan does not close prior to the lock-in expiration date for any reason whatsoever, including but not limited to reasons beyond the control of Alethes LLC, such as those related to appraisals, credit reports, mortgage payoffs, and title problems.

_____   _____
Applicant   Date   Applicant   Date

_____   _____
Applicant   Date   Applicant   Date

LOCK-IN AGREEMENT

Lock-in Date _____   Expiration Date _____

Loan Type _____   Mortgage Amount _____

** Re-Lock Date: _____   **** Re-Lock Expiration Date** _____

I/We acknowledge and understand that Alethes LLC has agreed and committed to a _____ interest rate, _____ discount point(s), and _____ origination fee on a mortgage loan amount of $ _____, pursuant to the purchase and financing of _____ (property address), for a period of _____ days from the date hereof. I/We understand that this interest rate and points are guaranteed by Alethes LLC, subject to loan approval, regardless of any change **up or down** in market interest rates. In consideration of this guarantee by Alethes LLC, I/we agree to close at these locked-in terms upon loan approval prior to the lock-in expiration date. I/We further acknowledge and agree that, in the event this LOCK-IN AGREEMENT expires, my/our loan will close at the expired interest rate and points or the prevailing market price, **whichever is greater**.

_____   _____
Applicant   Date   Applicant   Date

_____   _____
Applicant   Date   Loan Representative   Date

basis points during the course of a day. When you lock in your loan and get your confirmation, the loan officer could still try for *market gain*. Market gains are a little-known aspect—at least to consumers—of mortgage pricing. No surprise; they're a way for the loan officer to make a little more money off of you.

Let's say that you've been following rates for a while and have your loan application in at your chosen lender. When you hit your target rate, you call your loan officer and lock in. "Sure," says the loan officer, who has been watching mortgage bond trends over the past several days and thinks that rates might continue to move lower. So instead of locking you in "officially," he holds off, letting rates move downward, potentially making a little extra money.

For example, you lock in at 6 percent on a 20-year loan at $300,000 and no points for 30 days, with the loan officer making 1.25 percent YSP, or $3,750. But rates gradually move down over the next few days, and the loan officer watches that YSP grow to 1.75 percent. Now, the revenue to the loan officer is $5,250, and not $3,750. Is that legal? Yes. The loan officer is not obligated to give you the new lower rates. You have a lock agreement, remember? Just as you're protected with a lock agreement if rates move up, so are you "protected" when rates move down. You get what you get.

By the same token, your loan officer, who is waiting on locking in your loan in order to make a little extra money, might also be on the wrong side of things if rates, in fact, move up and not down. If you lock in at 6 percent, with the loan officer making $3,750, what if rates move in opposite favor of the loan officer, and the YSP goes from 1.25 percent, to perhaps .25 percent over the next few days? Now the loan officer is making only $750 (or $375, after splitting with her company). In that case, she made the wrong bet on interest rates.

I've seen loan officers who routinely operate in this fashion and lose more than they win. Why? They get greedy, much like an addicted gambler who wants to roll the dice "just one more time." But when he gets what he wants, he rolls yet again. Loan officers who work for market gains follow all the economic reports, subscribe to all the services, and don't sleep at night.

♦ ♦ ♦

Live mortgage-bond pricing isn't available to the general public. You can track other bonds or follow the 10-year Treasury bond, but it won't give you an exact reading of mortgage rates throughout the day. If rates have in fact moved 1/4 percent lower, you might be in line for a renegotiation for a new rate.

Let's say you followed rates for a while, found your lender, and locked in—only to watch rates continue to slide. What to do?

The first thing you do is call your loan officer and plead your case. But don't expect much sympathy if rates have moved only a few basis points, or even just 1/8 percent. Some won't budge at all unless rates have moved by more than 1/4 percent, though there is no universal rule. The only thing you can really do is to threaten to move your loan to another lender. This will often get the most attention. Just asking for a new lower rate won't cut it. If the rate move is less than 1/4 percent, don't expect the lender to budge. But if it does move more than that, the loan officer will likely work to get you the lower rate. After all, she has already worked hard on your file and won't make money unless the loan actually closes.

If you're working with a mortgage broker, the broker will contact another wholesale lender and lock you at the new lower rate. If you're working with a mortgage banker, the loan officer will contact the secondary department and request that they modify your loan lock. That's one disadvantage a banker does have when compared to a broker. Secondary departments are loath to break lock requests and issue new ones. Their thinking is, "We don't call your customer up and ask that they take a higher rate when rates go up. Why do they think we'll give them a lower rate when rates go down?" That's a logical response. But in reality, they're likely to lose the loan.

When you work with a banker, don't expect the absolute best interest-rate adjustment, if you've already locked. But you can get close. The best alternative would be to work with a banker who can also broker mortgage loans.

So, one question you should ask when interviewing loan officers: "What happens if rates move down after I lock in with you?" But the *real* question is: How do I know when to lock and when to wait? No one can predict the future. Sometimes, world events occur that not even the best market analyst can forecast. Let's say you're watching the economic reports and following mortgage rates, waiting for them to drop a little bit more so you can lock in at the "perfect" rate. And imagine, at the same time, that there's a major breakthrough in Middle East peace talks, coupled with the announcement of a new, inexpensive and environmentally safe fuel that will eliminate the world's dependence on oil. The world is no longer such a shaky place. Guess what happens, though? Investors pull money out of bonds and invest in the stock market, and your "perfect rate" is gone. That may be an extreme example, but the point is that nobody knows what rates are going to do because nobody knows what actually will happen in the future. One can make educated guesses, but no one really knows.

What happens when you wait? Let's say that you've done your homework on a mortgage loan and evaluated your recovery period. You've got a $400,000 mortgage, a hybrid, which has just adjusted to 7.50 percent, and you can refinance today on a 30-year fixed-rate loan at 6.25 percent. Your current payment on your $400,000 balance is now at $2,796, while refinancing into a 30-year note at 6.25 percent gives you a new monthly payment of $2,462, saving you $334 in interest.

You do your research, select the best loan officer you can find, and get a good rate. But you've been following the news lately, and it's possible that rates could continue to slide. After all, most every economic report that's being released shows continued weakness in the economy. And based on the most recent CPI number, there appears to be little inflation.

So you decide to wait a few more weeks. Rates move up a little and they move down a little. Overall, while you were waiting, they inched up another 1/8 percent to 6.375 percent. It's still a good idea at 6.375 percent because your recovery period is only nine months. But darn it, you had 6.25 percent right in your hands and you let it get away! The difference between 6.375 percent and 6.25 percent is only $33, but your goal was 6.25 percent and not 6.375 percent.

That's okay, though, you reason. Rates have got to come back down to 6.25 percent or better. After all, everyone is saying the Fed still has plenty of room to lower rates. So you wait a few more weeks and, sure enough, you get 6.25 percent again. It's been just over two months since you could have locked in at 6.25 percent. But you decide you're going to watch one more month's worth of economic reports, keep your fingers crossed, and have your loan officer's cell phone number at the ready when you decide to lock in.

The third month, alas, doesn't provide you with expected lower rates For each time one economic report is released showing a slowing economy, another report is released hinting the opposite. You can still get 6.25 percent, so you decide to lock in and move on. But by holding out for another $33 per month, you wasted three months' worth of interest at the old, higher rate of 7.50 percent. In fact, you'll have wasted a total of $1,003 in interest because you didn't want the 6.375 percent rate. That's $33-per-month difference between 6.25 percent and 6.375 percent, instead of the $334 you could have gotten when you first started the process. You just added $1,003 to save $33. If you divide the $1,003 by the $33 difference you wanted, that wait cost you $1,003 / $33 = 30 months.

Instead of trying to second-guess, set a target rate for your refinance. When you reach that target, lock it in. If rates continue to slide, say to 5.75 percent, you can always refinance all over again. That's a mathematical way to determine when to lock.

The other way takes a prudent approach.

Being prudent essentially means taking the safe path and minimizing risk. I feel as though I've been asked a million times, "What do you think rates are going to do, David?" I'm not really comfortable predicting interest rates. And I'm certainly not comfortable with giving such advice to clients. After all, it could backfire. I'd hate to tell people it's a good idea not to lock and then have rates continue to move up, never looking back. I always answer the rate forecast question this way: "I don't know where rates are headed, but my advice is for you to imagine that *whichever* decision you make turns out to be wrong. If so, which way would you rather be wrong?"

For example, if your goal were to get 6.25 percent and you got it and were wondering whether or not to lock, address your reaction as if you had, in theory, made the wrong choice. But what if you locked in, and rates moved down to 6.125 percent from your 6.25 percent initial goal, or if you decided *not* to lock in rates and they moved up and never looked back?

I thought so. If you're comfortable with 6.25 percent and your recovery period is in line, then go ahead and lock. There's nothing worse than having something available to you suddenly disappear.

Speaking of timing, is there a better part of the month in which to close? When you bought your property, your Realtor probably told you to close at the end of the month because it would save you a month. She would be right. The reason of course is that the later in the month you close, the less money you'll have to bring to the closing table in the form of prepaid interest.

But recall that in a refinance, you have both prepaid interest and interest in arrears. The interest in arrears is the per diem interest accruing at the old, higher rate, while prepaid interest at the new lower rate doesn't accrue until your new loan closes. The best time of the month to close a refinance is *as soon as you're able*. The longer you take to close a refinance, the more you're accruing in higher interest charges. And if you roll all your closing costs, including interest, into your new loan, it will also make your monthly payments higher. After all, you borrowed more.

It's also important that you stay vigilant during the loan process. If you have 30 days in which to close your loan, then you need to cooperate with your loan officer and get her whatever documentation she requests—and get it to her promptly. If it's day 20 of a 30-day lock, and you still haven't sent in your pay check stubs or provided requested copies of W2s, don't be surprised if your lock expires. If your lock expires before your loan closes, your loan will be subject to the worst-case scenario. That means if you lock in at 6 percent and rates drop to 5.75 percent and your 6 percent rate expires, you get the 6 percent rate, not the new lower 5.75 percent. If you lock in at 6 percent and rates move to 6.25 percent with an expired lock, you again get the higher rate at 6.25 percent.

Do lenders slow down your loan process *intentionally* so your lower rate will expire? During times of lower rates, refinance activity across the country goes up. More and more people apply for a refinance—so many that sometimes, lenders aren't staffed to handle the extra workload. That means things will slow down. It will take longer for appraisals and it will take longer for title insurance policies to be issued. It will also take longer for everything else in the loan approval process. But lenders don't purposefully slow a loan down to get another 1/8 percent. As rates move up for consumers, so too do they move up for lenders. Slowing down a loan approval on purpose doesn't make sense.

♦ CHAPTER SIX ♦

How to Save on Closing Costs

The key element when refinancing is the recovery period. And the closing costs affect the recovery period more than any other factor. Because a refinancing means replacing an old loan with a new loan, it means that a whole new set of closing costs arises. Some closing costs offer discounts, some you can negotiate away, while others are set in stone. To mix things up a bit, different parts of the country have their own rules on who pays what and what type of discounts may be available.

Here is a list of potential fees you may encounter and an approximate amount on what you can expect to pay.

Lender Fees

Discount Point	1% of the loan amount
Origination Fee	1% of the loan amount
Administration	$200–$300
Application	$200–$400
Appraisal	$300–$500; some lenders require two appraisals for jumbo loans
Credit Report	$10–$65
Flood Certificate	$17–$20

Processing	$300–$500
Tax Service	$60–$70
Underwriting	$300–$500

Nonlender Fees

Title Examination	$125–$200
Title Insurance	Varies by state; may range from $1 per thousand financed, to 1 percent of the loan amount
Attorney Fee	$225–$500
Abstract Fee	$50–$300
Document Prep	$100–$300
Document Stamp	1–3% of the loan amount
Escrow	$150–$350
Intangible Tax	1–3% of the loan amount
Recording	$50–$85
Settlement/Closing	$150–$350
Survey	$300–$500

That's a lot of fees. Note that this is a general list and those with experience in reviewing closing costs for real estate transactions would probably look at this list and say "Hey, that's too low!" or "Hey, that's too high!" and either way, they would be correct. These are general estimates of potential fees.

When you call a loan officer and get a rate quote, you'll also ask for a *Good Faith Estimate of Settlement Charges*, or simply a *good faith estimate.* A lender can have some of the lowest rates available but offset those low rates with high lender fees. (I told you it can be a shell game!) The good faith estimate is a list of all potential charges you may encounter during your refinance, divided into different sections, or "series." Each individual cost is associated with a "series number." For example, a discount point is line item 802, the appraisal is line item 803, and so on. But the key in reviewing good faith estimates from different lenders is to concentrate only on the *800 series of fees* and no one else's. Why? Because the lender has direct control over the 800 series, which includes appraisal charges, credit reporting charges, and various lender fees. Lenders don't have control of how much title insurance is (line item 1108) or what escrow fees are (line item 1101), so there's little use in taking those numbers into account when comparing lenders.

I'll give you an example of how lenders can mix the numbers up to make them appear to have a better offering. Say you get quotes from two lenders. Lender A offers 6 percent at no points, and Lender B offers 6.125 percent at no points. Lender A is your best deal, no? Wait a minute—you need to do some more homework.

Lender A's good faith estimate includes:

Appraisal	$350
Credit Report	$15
Processing	$400
Underwriting	$500
Administrative	$500
Application	$400
Total	$2,165

Lender B's good faith estimate includes:

Appraisal	$350
Credit Report	$15

Processing	$400
Total	$765

Now, who has the better deal? Yes, Lender A had the better rate, but also charged you $1,400 more in the process! I'll just bet that Lender B would be more than happy to hit you up front with more fees as well. That's why you need to compare not just the rate but also the fees.

You can also perform the same function by reviewing the APR given for that rate quote. The APR is the cost of your money borrowed, expressed as an annual rate. Did you get an interest rate with your mortgage? Of course you did, but you also got some other things as well that were required to close your loan. The lender needed an appraisal and a credit report, and also charged you some internal fees as well. You might have gotten your 6 percent rate but you must also factor in the additional $2,165 dollars.

The APR takes these additional costs and expresses them as an annual interest rate. The higher the APR, the more fees you've incurred. In the following example on a $100,000 loan amount and a 30-year fixed, the APRs for both lenders look like this:

Lender A

Note Rate	6%
Closing Costs	$2,165
APR	6.205

Lender B

Note Rate	6.125%
Closing Costs	$765
APR	6.197

Now compare the APRs for both loans. Lender A had the better note rate of 6 percent, but when closing fees were factored in, the APR was actually higher than the 6.125 percent note rate offered by Lender B. The difference between monthly payments in this example for both rates is only $8. Had you simply chosen the lower rate without regard for lender fees, you would have a recovery period of 175 months: $1,400 / $8.00 = 175.

APR is only effective when comparing the exact same loan program from different lenders. It doesn't work if you're comparing a 5/1 hybrid ARM to a 30-year fixed-rate, because you're working with two different indexes. That's another trick loan officers can use to lowball all the nonlender fees.

The loan officer has absolutely no control over the cost of title insurance. It is what it is. But too often, when people receive good faith estimates they just look at the bottom line figure: "Honey, these people charge $3,000, while these other people charge $3,500. Let's go with the cheaper ones!" That's a mistake.

Let's assume again that you got two good faith estimates from Lender A and Lender B. Lender A's good faith estimate includes:

Appraisal	$350
Credit Report	$15
Processing	$400
Underwriting	$500
Administrative	$500
Application	$400
Total	$2,165

Lender B's good faith estimate includes:

Appraisal	$350
Credit Report	$15
Processing	$400
Total	$765

But now you look at the nonlender charges, and you find some differences in several fee categories:

	Lender A	Lender B
Closing Fee	$50	$200
Document Fee	$50	$300
Attorney Fee	$75	$350
Title Insurance	$175	$1,500
Total Nonlender	$350	$2,350
Total Estimate	$2,575	$3,115

So you figure, "Hey, Lender A is a lot less expensive. I think I'll go with the slightly higher rate at Lender A. After all, the difference is only $8 per month and I'd rather do that than spend an additional $540. That's a 67-month recovery period!" So you go along on your merry way and tell Lender B, "Thanks, but no thanks."

A couple of weeks later, you head to your closing, sit down at the closing table, and see that something is very, very wrong. The closing fee isn't $50, but $200, and the attorney fee isn't $75, but $350. It's time to call Lender A and find out what's going on—and fast—because rates have moved up since you locked in, and if you don't sign today, you'll lose that great rate. You call your loan officer and say, "What gives with the higher fees?" and he says, "I sent you an estimate; I have no control over what third parties charge." You're stuck. You either cancel the loan or sign. So you decide it's better to swallow hard and keep the low rates, all the while knowing you got snookered.

Do loan officers do this? You bet. Not all of them, just the bad ones. And not all loan officers are bad. But you do need to understand that when comparing lenders, you should be concerned with lender charges only, not third-party charges.

Negotiating Closing Costs

There are, in fact, closing costs you can get discounts on with a refinance, some from the lender and some from the nonlenders. Let's first look at lender charges.

Lenders not only charge their rate and points, but they also can have additional charges many simply call *junk fees*. Lenders can charge as many fees as they can get away with, but they have to be competitive in their marketplace. In certain parts of the country, a loan-processing fee is standard. In other parts, it is not. Underwriting is a common fee and can vary in price, depending on the locale. Lenders can also mix up their fees to make them appear better. You need to know how this trick is done.

Let's look at Lender A and Lender B again. Both are quoting 6 percent, with no points.

	Lender A	*Lender B*
Appraisal	$350	$350
Credit	$15	$15
Processing	$400	$400

Underwriting	$400	-0-
Administrative	-0-	$400
Total	$1,165	$1,165

Lenders aren't required to have an administrative fee or a processing fee; they can have as many different fees as they want. Often, you can contact two different lenders and hear one loan officer say something like, "Our fees are competitive, and we don't charge an underwriting fee." Maybe not. But he *does* charge an administrative fee that Lender A does not. Or still another says, "We waive our normal $400 underwriting charge and we also waive our $500 mortgage broker fee. That's $900 in savings!"

Wow, that's a lot, isn't it? No, not if they never charge it in the first place. It's easy to waive a fee if it's never charged at all. Pay no attention to the *name* of the fee, but pay careful attention to what those fees *add up to*. Remember that loan officers get paid on commission. That includes the lender fees as well. So if the loan officer can charge you a $400 underwriting fee, it means she'll make another $200 after splitting it with her employer.

Sometimes, loan officers will have a *throwaway fee* that they can use in the negotiation process. (A lender can have two types of fees: throwaways and required.) A throwaway fee might be a processing fee, something that's nice to get from the borrower but is not a required fee from their employer. So you may hear, "Say, if you lock in with me today, I'll waive that $400 processing fee. What do you say?" Mortgage companies have fixed costs to run their business. They pay for salaries, desks, chairs, and computers, just like any other business. And just like any other business, they'll try to make as much as they can on each transaction, while keeping competitive.

A lender who charges $1,000 more than the competition for the very same loan won't be in business for long. But if a lender has closing fees in line with the competition, it's likely those fees will be similar, if not the name.

As part of a loan officer's compensation agreement, she might have the ability to waive a particular fee without taking the hit, but she can't waive another fee unless she pays for it herself. This is the difference between a throwaway fee and a required one.

Let's say you're negotiating with your loan officer for your best deal and you say, "If you waive your processing fee and your administrative fee, I'll do business with you today." So the loan officer does some calculations. Your loan amount of $100,000 at 6 percent gives $1,350 in income, plus $400 for processing and $400 in administrative costs. The administrative fee is a throwaway, but the processing fee is not. By waiving the throwaway fee, the commission works like this:

Income	$1,350
Administrative	($400)
Total	$950
Commission (50%)	$475

The loan officer may think about waiving the processing fee, but if loan officers routinely made $475 on every mortgage they produced, they'd soon be out of business.

By waiving the throwaway and the required fee, the commission works differently. The administrative is a throwaway and the loan officer doesn't have to pay for it, but while the loan officer can waive the processing fee just to get the deal, the math is hard to work:

Income	$1,350
Administrative	($400)
Subtotal	$950
Processing	($400)
Total	$550
Commission (50%)	$275

This is nearly working for free, and the loan officer wouldn't likely take this deal. But you never know, so you have to ask.

Another common fee is the origination charge. This lender charge is expressed as a percentage of the loan amount. The origination fee is normally 1 percent of the loan. It goes straight to the lender, unlike a discount point that is used to reduce a mortgage rate. Origination fees are also negotiable, but often in exchange for a higher or lower rate, much like a discount point is charged. It's also another reason why origination charges, along with discount points, are tax-deductible items, whereas the remaining closing costs are not.

As long as the origination fee is expressed as a percentage of the loan, it may be treated the same way as a tax deduction, but only over the term of the loan. If you get a 30-year fixed-rate and pay a 1 percent origination fee on a $300,000 note, or $3,000, then you may deduct 1/30 of that $3,000, or $100, from that particular tax year, each year until the loan is retired. If you pay off that loan early and don't take it to full term, then when you pay off that loan, the remaining balance may be deducted, just as a discount point is on a refinance.

Other areas where you may be able to negotiate fees:

Appraisals. It's possible to get a reduced fee from an appraiser, say from $350 to $295. But you'll have to ask for it up front. The best way to get an appraisal fee reduced is to first get your loan approved by your lender, and then see if you can get an appraisal waived completely or partially. When a loan is submitted through an automated underwriting system, stronger loan files by way of credit, income, and equity can get processed easier with lower costs. One of these lower costs is the appraisal. A full appraisal (including an inspection of both the inside and outside of the structure) may cost around $350. Another category of appraisals is sometimes called the *drive-by* appraisal, where the appraiser doesn't have to physically inspect the property. Instead, he drives by and makes a visual inspection from the street, essentially ensuring there's actually a house there and that it's not falling down. A drive-by appraisal costs about $200. Finally, there is a complete waiver: if you have more than 20 percent equity in your home, your credit is in good standing, and your debt-to-income levels are in line, it's likely you'll get your appraisal fee waived, reducing your recovery period.

Survey. A survey is a map of your property showing your property lines and where your structure sits on the property. It also shows sidewalks and other *easements,* such as electrical and utility lines. An easement is a previous right to access your property. Common easements are from the telephone company, which has a right to your backyard if that's where their equip-ment rests and they need to fix it. Many lenders will take a copy of your old survey, as long as nothing has changed since you bought the property (for example, taking down a fence or adding a swimming pool or garage). Surveys can cost upwards of $500, so it's important to keep your initial survey in a safe place in case you need it later.

Title Insurance. Title insurance is an insurance policy that protects the lender and the borrowers from previous claims on the property that went unrecorded or previous interests that weren't properly cleared. Title insurance can be expensive—as much as 1 percent of the loan amount—but you may be able to get a discount. Be careful with these discounts, sometimes called *reissues*. The rules for qualifying for discounts can vary from state to state. Certain states only give you a discount if you use the very same title insurance company. Other states don't care if you use another insurance company, but will discount based on the age of the current title insurance policy. Title insurance dis-counts can reach 50 percent, depending on the area. This may well be your biggest single savings in a refinance transaction.

Escrow or Settlement Fee. This is the fee paid to your closer for handling your loan closing. You may be able to negotiate a discount, if you've used your closer previously. You may also get a discount from your escrow agent, if you use affiliated services from the escrow company. In California, for example, most title insurance companies also own or have business relationships with escrow companies. If you use their title insurance company and close with their escrow company, you may get double discounts. That could save you hundreds of dollars.

Attorney. Negotiating a discount with an attorney has a lot to do with the function he performs in the state where he practices. In California, there are no attorneys required for a real estate transaction. In Chicago, you might get a discount with the attorney handling your closing, if you also use his title insurance. In Texas, where attorneys are responsible for reviewing loan documents, it's the lender who works with attorneys for document review, even though it's the consumer who ultimately pays for the service. The fee can't be negotiated.

Government Fees. Government fees range from property taxes to recording fees and document stamps. As much as one would like to negotiate with the government, when it comes to real estate, there's no room for haggling.

There are two types of fees: *recurring* and *nonrecurring*. When evaluating closing costs, the recurring costs matter little. But the nonrecurring ones matter a lot. A recurring closing cost is one that occurs again and again, while a nonrecurring closing cost only applies one time, in direct correlation with the refinance closing. Recurring closing costs are interest charges, insurance, and property taxes. Nonrecurring closing costs are fees such as appraisal charges, attorney fees, and any other item associated with that refinance transaction. The reason you should disregard recurring costs is that you will pay them, regardless of a refinance. You will pay your insurance policy and you will pay your taxes, as well as interest payments to the lender. But when evaluating closing costs and recovery periods, adding recurring fees into the mix messes up the calculation. So you can forget about adding those into your recovery period mix.

Origination Charges and Discount Points

Let's look a little further into origination charges and discount points. Origination fees are most often charged by mortgage brokers, but don't necessarily have to be. Furthermore, in certain parts of the country, origination fees are unheard of. That doesn't mean loans are automatically cheaper when an origination fee isn't charged. That's because either the rate will increase or a point will be charged instead. But for purposes of comparing whether or not to pay them, origination charges and points are synonymous, when calculating recovery periods.

Discount points drop your rate by 1/4 percent for each point paid. Let's say the loan amount = $300,000.

Rate	Points	$$	Payment
7%	-0-	-0-	$1,995
6.875%	½	$1,500	$1,970
6.75%	1	$3,000	$1,945
6.625%	1½	$4,500	$1,920
6.50%	2	$6,000	$1,896

You'll notice that for each 1/8 percent difference in rate, the payment goes up or down by about $25 per month. If you paid 1 point, or $3,000, then you would save $50 per month when you compare the payment at 7 percent and the one at 6.75 percent. But you had to pay the $3,000 privilege in order to get that lower rate. What's the recovery period for that $3,000?

$$\$3,000 / \$50 = 60 \text{ months}$$

Good idea? Probably not. You'll find that if, in fact, you're getting a true $^1/_4$ percent reduction in rate for each point paid, then four to five years is a common recovery period, and that seems to me to be a long time. Technically, one should be living in the house long enough to recover the closing costs, but in reality, five years is a long time. You could take that same $3,000 and put it away in a mutual fund or bond, or use it to pay down your principal.

If, in fact, you intend to keep the new loan to full term, then by paying down the principal by $3,000 you're ahead of the game, when comparing it to paying points. If you pay $3,000 to lower your payment by $25 over the course of the loan, you saved $9,000. If you took that same $3,000 and immediately applied it to principal, you would have saved just over $20,000 in interest charges.

I've never been a big fan of paying discount points or origination charges when acquiring a mortgage loan. The math just never seems to work out in the favor of the borrower.

The No-Closing-Cost Refinance

Want to speed up your recovery period? How about zero months? How about refinancing your loan to whatever term or rate you want, and also pay no closing costs whatsoever? You've heard the radio ads; you've seen the television and Internet pitches about no-closing-cost loans from mortgage brokers you've never heard of, as well as from some of the country's biggest banks.

But the fact is *nobody* works for free. The attorney still has to be paid, and the title insurance as well. So how does this work? First, pay attention to the fine print.

A popular lender who frequently advertises on television had a long-running ad that said "No Closing Costs!" along with fast-scrolling fine print—too small and too swift for the average human being to read. What the fine print said was that "No Closing Costs!" meant "No Lender Fees." Big difference. The lender generated a lot of business with this particular advertisement. When consumers called the toll-free number, the customer service representative would explain that it was not, in fact, a "No Closing Costs *Whatsoever*" loan. Soon, people began to complain, and the ad was changed to: "No Lender Fees!" If you see such an ad, make sure you're clear on exactly which fees the lender is talking about.

But there are no-closing-cost loans. Most anyone can offer them. It just takes a bit of math to make sure it works for you.

Remember how one discount point will reduce your interest rate by about 1/4 percent? Conversely, if you increase your interest rate by 1/4 percent, suddenly you have 1 point available to use to apply to your closing costs—sort of like paying points in reverse. The point coming to you is made available through the yield spread premium, or YSP. The higher the rate, the more the YSP. Lenders can offer no-closing-cost loans by getting more YSP while increasing your interest rate just enough to cover closing costs, as well as having the lender make a little money.

You can already see that the "No Closing Cost" mantra is really a misnomer. There *is* a cost; it's just expressed as a higher rate. You pay for that each and every month with a higher payment. It's up to you to see if it makes sense in your case.

Let's look at an example of closing costs on a typical loan.

Appraisal	$350
Credit	$15
Processing	$400
Underwriting	$350
Escrow	$200
Title Insurance	$585
Attorney	$100
Documents	$200
Recording	$100
Document Stamp	$500
Total	$2,800

This loan carries $2,800 of nonrecurring closing costs, and the interest rate is at 7 percent for a 30-year fixed-rate loan on a $200,000 mortgage. By taking the total closing costs of $2,800 and dividing them by the mortgage amount of $200,000, you get .014, or 1.4 points.

If your rate with zero points is 7 percent and you can "buy up" your rate by ¹/₄ percent with 1 point, then by increasing your interest rate to 7.25 percent, you get 1 point credit to you from the lender. By increasing it just a tad more to 7.375 percent, you get 1.5 points credited to you at closing, or a $3,000 credit. Yes, your rate went up but you didn't have to pay any closing costs. Your monthly payment went from $1,330 per month to $1,381. That's a difference of $51.

If your old interest rate was at 7.50 percent with a payment of $1,398, and you refinanced into a 7.375 percent rate, you dropped your monthly payment by only $17, but you did it for free. Or at least you offset the closing costs and your recovery period is zero. But would you refinance for $17? Probably not. Would you refinance if you had an ARM that was about to adjust much higher than 7.375 percent? Of course. Would you refinance if your goal were to reduce the term and it didn't cost you anything? Sure.

Let's look at another example. Everything is the same, except now the loan amount is $500,000, instead of $200,000.

Appraisal	$350
Credit	$15
Processing	$400
Underwriting	$350
Escrow	$200
Title Insurance	$585
Attorney	$100
Documents	$200
Recording	$100
Document Stamp	$500
Total	$2,800

Divide $2,800 by the new higher loan amount of $500,000, and the answer is .006, or .6 points. That's only about 1/8 percent in rate. Now you only have to increase your note rate from 7 percent to 7.125 percent, instead of 7 percent to 7.375 percent. The monthly payment at 7.50 percent on $500,000 is $3,496. At 7 percent and 7.125 percent, the payments are $3,326 and $3,368, or $42 per month. The difference between $3,496 and

$3,368, for the no-closing-cost refinance, is $128. Again, your recovery period is zero. Would you refinance, for "free," to save $128? Yes.

The difference in both the rate needed to cover the closing costs and the difference in monthly payments is due to the size of the loan. When we changed loan amounts from $200,000 to $500,000, we didn't need such a large rate spread to cover the closing costs.

Let's do this one more time, only with a smaller loan amount of $75,000.

Appraisal	$350
Credit	$15
Processing	$400
Underwriting	$350
Escrow	$200
Title Insurance	$585
Attorney	$100
Documents	$200
Recording	$100
Document Stamp	$500
Total	$2,800

Divide $2,800 by $75,000, and the answer is .037, or 3.7 points. Now you need to increase the rate by nearly a full percentage point to cover the closing costs. That means the rate would go from the 7 percent you could get with no points to 8 percent, with no points or closing costs. Would you refinance a loan to increase the rate from 7.50 percent to 8 percent with no closing costs? Of course not.

No-closing-cost loans are a function of the closing costs, the loan amount, and the rate. The lower the loan amount, the more the rate will have to increase to cover closing fees. That's because closing costs are expressed as a percentage of the loan amount.

Another way to soften the blow of closing costs is not to pay them, but to *borrow* them. A unique advantage to refinancing a loan versus a purchase mortgage is that with a refinance, you can roll closing costs in with your loan amount, instead of writing a check for them. In fact, this is the most common way people deal with closing costs during a refinance.

Let's look at a couple of examples to see the impact of financing costs into the loan.

Appraisal	$350
Credit	$15
Processing	$400
Underwriting	$350
Escrow	$200
Title Insurance	$585
Attorney	$100
Documents	$200
Recording	$100
Document Stamp	$500
Total	$2,800

On a loan amount of $200,000, you would need to increase the loan to cover the closing costs to $202,800. A 7 percent, 30-year payment would be $1,349. If you paid the $2,800 out of your pocket, your monthly payment on $200,000 at 7 percent would be $1,330. When you compare the no-closing-cost loan at 7.375 percent on $200,000, the payment goes to $1,381.

Closing Costs Paid	Loan Amount	Monthly Payment
Out of Pocket	$200,000	$1,330
Rolled into the Loan	$202,800	$1,349
No-Closing-Cost Loan	$200,000	$1,381

Let's look at the same example, using the higher loan amount of $500,000.

Appraisal	$350
Credit	$15
Processing	$400
Underwriting	$350
Escrow	$200
Title Insurance	$585
Attorney	$100
Documents	$200
Recording	$100
Document Stamp	$500
Total	$2,800

On a loan amount of $500,000, you would need to increase the loan to cover the closing costs to $502,800. A 7 percent, 30-year payment would be $3,345. If you paid the $2,800 out of your pocket, your monthly payment on $500,000 at 7 percent would be $3,326. When you compare the no-closing-cost loan at 7.125 percent on $500,000, the payment goes to $3,368.

Closing Costs Paid	Loan Amount	Monthly Payment
Out of Pocket	$500,000	$3,326
Rolled into the Loan	$502,800	$3,345
No-Closing-Cost Loan	$500,000	$3,368

The higher the loan amount, the more attractive the no-closing-cost. A no-closing-cost loan should also be considered when you originally purchase a piece of property. Say you are exploring a rate-and-term refinance, and the rates drop. If you paid points and closing costs for the acquisition, you're already behind in your recovery period.

Let's look at an example, using a $500,000 loan for the purchase.

Points	$5,000
Appraisal	$350
Credit	$15
Processing	$400
Underwriting	$350
Escrow	$200
Title Insurance	$585
Attorney	$100
Documents	$200
Recording	$100
Document Stamp	$500
Total	$7,800

When you acquired the property, rates were at 7.50 percent with 1 point. But six months later, rates have dropped to 6.50 percent, so you consider a refinance. You could have gotten 7.75 percent with no points, but you chose the rate with points. One point of $5,000 would drop your payment from $3,852 to $3,496, or $356 per month. Your point recovery period is $5,000/ $356 = 14 months.

But six months later, after you purchased the property, you decide to refinance. And guess what? That point you paid only saved you six months' worth of savings, or $2,136.

$5,000 − $2,136 = $2,864

You'll never get that back because your loan didn't last long enough to reach its recovery period. If rates went from 7.50 percent to 6.50 percent, the difference in the monthly payment in this example is $3,496 − $3,160 = $336.

Again, using the same example:

Appraisal	$350
Credit	$15
Processing	$400
Underwriting	$350
Escrow	$200
Title Insurance	$585
Attorney	$100
Documents	$200
Recording	$100
Document Stamp	$500
Total	$2,800

The recovery period is 8.8 months: $2,800 / $316 = 8.8. If you increased your rate to cover the $2,800 in closing costs, it would look like this: $2,800 / $500,000 = .006, or about 5/8 of a point, or about a 3/8 percent increase in rate. And consider that 6.875 percent on $500,000 over 30 years = $3,284 per month. On a no-closing-cost loan, the difference between a 7.50 percent and a 6.875 percent rate is $3,496 − $3,284 = $212, and zero recovery period.

A no-closing-cost loan also needs to be looked at in terms of interest rate cycles. Interest rates will move in cycles from high, to low, to medium, then to high again. When evaluating which rate to take, it's important to take a look and see where rates are when you refinance, compared to where they've been over the previous few years. One of the best websites to track historical interest rate data can be found at www.hsh.com.

If you see that interest rates are at relative highs when you finance a property, you want to keep your closing costs, especially points, as low as possible while keeping an eye on future interest rates, should they slide back down. If rates are at relative lows, consider paying a point and competitive closing costs when you finance your property. Your loan officer should help guide you on this as well.

CHAPTER SEVEN

Predatory Lending, Loan Fraud, and Bad Guys

What Is a Predatory Lender?

First, it's not necessarily a subprime lender. Consumer advocates sometimes bandy about the terms "predatory" and "subprime" as synonymous, but they're not. Any loan can be predatory, if the loan officer makes it so. The Senate, Congress, state governments, and a lot of consumer groups have tried to define predatory lending, but all the definitions I've seen are typical government gobbledygook or reactionary language.

There is no official government definition of *predatory*, but mine is probably the best. Federal and state bureaucracies take heed:

> **"A predatory loan is designed to do nothing but make the loan officer more money at the borrower's expense."**
>
> **—David Reed**

Thank you very much.

Subprime loans have higher rates, but that doesn't mean the lender is a predator. It simply means the lender is offsetting a greater risk with higher interest. Conventional loans do the very same thing, and they aren't predatory by nature. A conventional loan with 30 percent down will have a lower rate than a conventional loan with zero down. When lenders take a greater risk, regardless of loan type, the lender charges more in rate. If that lender didn't adjust for risk, it wouldn't be a very prudent lender—or be in business for very long. Loans by themselves aren't predatory. But loan officers can take a loan and turn it into one that charges excessive fees and rates, while stripping homeowners of their equity.

Here's an example of a predatory process.

Year 1

A single mom, recently divorced, inherits the home to raise her daughter. She also inherits the mortgage that goes along with it. She can pay the note, but occasionally has some trouble doing so. Her ex-husband, who is responsible for paying support, sometimes also has problems paying his bills. The current mortgage balance is $100,000 and the appraised value of the home, according to the appraisal done for the purposes of the divorce proceedings, is $200,000. The ex-husband can't pay his support payments, yet the wife still has to pay the mortgage. Soon, she gets behind on her bills, and she sees an advertisement that says "Cash in on your home equity and pay off your bills fast!"

The advertised loan was nothing out of the ordinary—a 2/28 subprime hybrid, perhaps the most common of all subprime loans.

She has about $30,000 in bills from previous student loans, a credit card, and an auto loan. If she paid off all of those, she would be able to pay just the house payment and relieve herself of all those extra bills. She contacted the mortgage company that advertised paying all her bills with a refinance, got a new loan for $130,000, and went on her merry way.

Year 2

This same woman got a phone call from the same loan officer who refinanced her initial cash-out refinance and asked how she was doing. She said she was doing fine, and the loan officer asked if she would like some extra cash to help out around the house, to buy a new car, or to help with everyday expenses. And he could do the very same thing that he did for her in Year 1, but this time with no closing costs. Not only could he do it with no closing costs—he could also reduce her monthly payments at the same time, if she took another hybrid mortgage. A hybrid would give her a lower rate, yet she would need to refinance in a couple of years to avoid the adjustment. But the loan officer would refinance her again, with no closing costs, to her original rate if, of course, rates remained the same.

The now ex-wife had a higher loan payment, her ex-husband still couldn't afford to pay his required spousal payments, and the loan officer knows this all along. So, she refinances yet again and borrows another $30,000, with a hybrid mortgage. The loan balance is about $160,000 at this point, and the appraised value is still at $200,000. And the monthly payments are still higher.

So, the loan officer makes about $2,000 every time the ex-wife refinances her mortgage to pay off her debts.

Year 3

Now, she can't make her payments. They're too high. She calls the loan officer yet again.

"I can't make my mortgage payment! Can you help?"

"Sure. I've been waiting for your call. Let's take out another cash-out refinance and pay off all your bills!"

Again, the woman, who couldn't afford her home in the first place due to her ex's inability to make his support payments, lost not just her home but the $100,000 in equity she had when she was awarded the home during the divorce proceedings.

Ka-ching! The loan officer has made nearly $10,000 from one person, whom he really doesn't care about. And do you think this is the only person this loan officer has done this to? Doubt it. It's called *equity stripping*. The unfortunate woman not only lost her equity, but she lost her home because of a predatory loan officer. The loan wasn't predatory; the loan officer *was*. He couldn't care less about his client's well-being. He was interested only in her pocketbook.

♦ ♦ ♦

Any legitimate loan can be made predatory, and believe it or not, mortgage loans aren't designed from the wheels up to take away someone's home. You might hear differently from consumer groups or read that in the newspaper, but lenders are in the lending business and not in the real estate business, meaning that they want mortgages and not to foreclose on homes and end up owning the property themselves, instead of collecting mortgage payments on those homes.

When a property is stripped of its equity and the lender owns the house, what will the lender then do with that house? Sell it? If there is no equity in the home, even if it sells for full value, the lender is automatically upside-down and actually loses money due to the costs associated with selling real estate. In fact, often the lender doesn't know a loan is predatory until it's too late.

Mortgage brokers make money by finding a loan and matching a lender with a borrower. The lender or the borrower pays the broker, and the loan is sent to the lender. It's the lender, not the mortgage broker, who approves or denies a mortgage application. As long as the loan meets the lender's guidelines in terms of credit, loan-to-value, and debt ratios, the lender approves the loan.

What the lender won't know is that the mortgage broker is slowly siphoning off any remaining equity in a property through systematic refinances. Each time the refinance is closed, the broker makes more money. This frustrates the lender as well because when a loan is refinanced, it's taken off the lender's books, and the lender no longer collects interest on the loan. But the mortgage broker couldn't care less about a foreclosure. He's already made his money.

Prepayment Penalties

Finding the best loan means you also have to watch out for certain things not necessarily disclosed up front when you first begin to explore refinance loan options. Prepayment penalties must be paid to the lender in case you pay off the mortgage early or pay extra on it as you go along. These penalties are typically found on subprime loan programs and can sometimes appear on other types of loans.

Why are there prepayment penalties on some loans? Sometimes, lenders want a guaranteed return on a mortgage loan. A lender could charge a higher rate, more fees, or they can apply a prepayment penalty—they'll get a certain percentage each month, until their desired income is met. If the loan pays off early, either by a refinance or by the owner selling the home, the lender still makes its money in the form of a prepayment penalty.

There are two types of prepayment penalties: hard and soft.

A *hard prepayment penalty* is a stern one. You absolutely may not pay anything extra toward the mortgage, nor may you pay it off for a predetermined period of time. If your monthly payment is $1,000, you may not pay $1,100 or your penalty kicks in. Prepayment penalties can vary with the lender, but the most common penalty is six months' worth of interest. If your monthly interest is $1,000 and you paid an extra $100 just one time, your prepayment penalty would kick in and you would owe the lender $6,000.

A *soft prepayment penalty* is kinder to you. It allows you to make some extra payments when you want, as long as whatever amount you pay doesn't exceed 20 percent of the outstanding principal balance. On a $100,000 mortgage, you could, theoretically, pay $20,000 extra without penalty. Soft penalties also don't apply if you happen to sell the property and not refinance the note. They also typically ask for six months' worth of interest if you refinance the note or pay more than 20 percent of the mortgage balance.

Prepayment penalties can sometimes be bought out up front by paying the lender a fee. Typical prepayment buyouts range from $1/2$ to 2 points up front. Two points on $100,000 is $2,000. If you have the option of buying out your prepayment penalty, be realistic about your situation. If you are taking a subprime loan and you have damaged credit, will you, in fact, repair your credit in time before you pay off the loan? Credit begins to fix itself in about two years; it won't happen overnight. So be certain that if you do buy out your prepayment penalty, you have a clear strategy. Otherwise, you'll be out $2,000.

There are also partial buyouts to fit the loan selected. Prepayment penalties typically last as long as the initial fixed period on the hybrid selected. If not, then you need to adjust the hybrid so they coincide. If you've got a 3/27 hybrid, you then need a three-year or less prepayment penalty period. With a 2/28, you'll want a two-year prepayment penalty.

If you've worked so hard to repair your credit so that you can refinance out of a subprime loan, only to find out you still can't refinance because of an onerous penalty, it will be a bad surprise.

Bad Guys

The mortgage business, like many others, has its own language. In the pursuit of getting the best mortgage loan at the best price for your specific circumstance, it's easy to gloss over words like "negative," "prepayment," or "annual percentage rate." And the bad guys in the business *want* you to gloss over them. In fact, they'll likely tell you they're not important.

I recall a woman who sent me an e-mail telling me a sad story, asking if I could help. Unfortunately I could not.

While she was still working, she had bought a condominium in Florida, where she planned to retire. The way she figured it, her retirement and pension were enough to pay her mortgage payment every month. The loan officer she found was a bad guy, but she didn't know it. The loan officer put her in a payment option ARM, pointing to the fact that her interest rate could be as low as 2 percent, and she could pay extra on the loan anytime she wanted.

What the loan officer did *not* explain is the negative amortization feature of the loan. Instead, he kept pointing to the 2 percent rate. She didn't understand it, but took the loan anyway. In fact, on the day of her closing, she saw that the rate on the loan was closer to 8 percent, not 2 percent. She called the broker from her cell phone and complained that her rate was wrong. He assured her that while 8 percent was on the paperwork, she still had the option of paying the 2 percent. While still not fully understanding the loan program and afraid of losing her condo, she went ahead and signed the paperwork.

A year and a half later, after she was already retired, she found out that she no longer had the 2 percent option, but only the 8 percent. She had to pull money out of her retirement account to make the full payment each month because her retirement wasn't enough to take care of her everyday living expenses. Her loan amortized negatively to the point where it was greater than when she first took out the mortgage. I suggested a refinance, but she said her loan balance was more than the value of the property, so she couldn't. She was going to have to let the property go into foreclosure. She lost her condo, severely damaged her credit, and had no place to live. All because of a bad guy.

How much is too much to pay in points or origination fees? I think if you pay anything more than 2 points, you're working with a bad guy. Discount points are supposed to do one thing and one thing only: buy down the interest rate. If you're getting quoted 6 percent with 2 points, then you need to ask what the points are for 6.25 percent, and the answer should be 1.

If you're paying points and you don't get any adjustment in rate, you're being taken advantage of. Loan officers can charge whatever they can legally get away with. Sometimes you might hear, "Well, this is a special loan program," or "Your loan was hard to do." That's hogwash. Lenders don't make loans that charge more because they're harder or charge more for a special loan program. There certainly are special programs, but if it's a higher risk to the lender, the lender increases the rate, not the points.

Paying points should be an option and not a requirement on the borrower's part. The lender will make money on the loan for the long term in the form of monthly payments, while the mortgage broker only makes money when the loan closes.

Lenders can also make money by selling a loan, either in bulk (when a bunch of loans are pooled together) or individually. A $100,000 mortgage at 8 percent is worth $164,155 in interest over and above the original $100,000 principal. That's a lot of money. A lender can sell a loan to get money from it right away, or he can simply wait for the money to come in monthly installments in the form of interest. When a lender charges you a point to lower your rate, that lender is also decreasing the amount of interest he'll collect on that note. It's suddenly less valuable over the long term.

There's really nothing wrong with paying points, but you need to be aware of the tradeoff. Anything more than a point should be looked at very carefully. And if a no-point loan isn't even offered, beware.

Bad guys brag about how much they made off of a client. I actually recall listening to a conversation among a group of young mortgage brokers at a convention. They were going back and forth about how much they were making off of their clients. I finally said, "Why do you screw your customers that way?" And one of them said, "Because we *can*, that's why." I felt like I needed to take a shower after listening to that bunch. It was almost as if it were a contest to see who could screw his customers the most.

When people get themselves into trouble financially and find that they need a subprime refinance to pay off debts, they're easy prey. The mortgage business is confusing. The consumer is thinking about getting out of a jam and not the terms of the mortgage. And loan officers know that. Bad guys can come across as saviors who have come to help you out of your situation. There are companies that sell "leads" to loan officers and, often, these leads come from a website somewhere, promising financing for people with bad credit. When a loan officer gets one of those leads, he'll reach out and begin working on you. He'll say things like, "We specialize in situations like yours," and "We're really glad we found you. No one but us can do your loan!"

If, in fact, you are a subprime borrower, it is imperative to get multiple quotes from different lenders. Don't fall for the "We're the only ones who can do this loan" line. The fact is, if you qualify for a subprime loan at one lender, you'll qualify for a subprime loan at another. Trust me—bad guys are everywhere. I can't stress how important it is to find a good loan officer.

Loan Fraud

There are two types of loan fraud: one where you *do* know about it, and one where you *don't* know about it. Loan fraud is a felony. People go to prison for it. Often, someone committing loan fraud does it by inflating his income a little just to qualify for a home loan. This only works on "stated" income loans, where the income is listed on the loan application but not verified with pay stubs or other means. Rarely is this done without the loan officer either knowing about it or suggesting it.

Loan programs have different qualification features. One of the most important is the *housing debt ratio,* which is the principal, interest, tax, and insurance payment (PITI) divided by the gross monthly income.

If a PITI payment on a house is $2,000 and the gross monthly income is $5,000, then the ratio is $2,000 / $5,000 = .40 or 40 percent. If the income loan the borrower is trying to qualify for has a maximum debt ratio of 40, the borrower would qualify for that loan from a debt ratio standpoint. If, however, the loan were a little larger or the rate were a little higher, and the PITI were raised to $2,200, then using the same income of $5,000, the ratio would be $2,200 / $5,000 = .44 or 44 percent. The loan requiring a maximum 40 debt ratio would be declined.

Guess what happens? The loan officer calls and says, "I know of a loan program that doesn't verify income, so if you just put more income on your application, we could get approved. The maximum debt ratio on this program is 40, so you'd need to put $5,500 on your loan application and we'd qualify." And the key part: "Don't worry, it's a stated-income loan, and they don't verify it anyway." So you take the advice of the loan officer, change the loan application, and *Voila*! Loan approval! And the loan officer was right; lenders don't verify income on a stated-income loan. You go along your merry way and everything's just fine. At least not if anything goes wrong.

If your loan officer told you to inflate your income in order to get a loan approval, you can bet you're not the only one he's done that with. And sooner or later, one of those loans he closed could very well have gone bad. After all, regardless of what type of income is put on the application, you still have to pay the mortgage, right? If the income were inflated beyond the point where the borrower could pay on a regular basis, then the loan could possibly go bad. When a loan goes bad, the lender then has a department that helps determine what happened. Did someone lose his job? Was there a bankruptcy? A divorce? What happened?

Let's take a step back and remember your closing. Do you recall a form called the IRS Form 4506? Whether or not you remember the 4506, you signed one. It allows a lender to pull tax returns directly from the IRS at some point down the road. And they *will* pull them in cases like this. They'll compare the income you put on your loan application with the income you filed with the IRS. If there's a difference, you could get into a lot of trouble—serious trouble. Stated loans are sometimes called "liar's loans" by some in the mortgage industry. It's obvious why they earned that nickname. Why did lenders invent them in the first place? To accommodate borrowers and make more loans.

Sometimes, people get paid irregularly or have complicated income streams—freelancers, for instance, or individuals with two or three part-time jobs. Certain loan programs may not allow income from part-time work. It's not that the income isn't there; it's just that it can't be used for qualifying purposes. There's a big difference between stating income that is there and stating income that's not there. The former is loan fraud.

At other times, loan fraud can be committed in much the same fashion by loan officers who change the application without even telling the customer. While you might not notice an incremental increase in your stated income—say from $5,000 to $5,100 a month—you would surely notice a more substantial increase to $7,000. And you could be complicit. Loan officers can fudge the numbers in an attempt to get you qualified. Let me re-phrase that: loan officers can fudge the numbers so they can get a *paycheck*. Bad guys couldn't care less about your personal situation. They only care that the deal closes.

Don't put yourself in a desperate situation. Don't do business with loan officers who suggest that you do things that aren't legal.

Epilogue

When you combine hard-to-decipher mortgage terminology with the baffling process of paying off an old loan and replacing it with a new one (not to mention adding to the mix a loan officer or two who can't wait to make money off you), things can quickly get pretty confusing. Refinancing has its own motivations that are different from a purchase. When you get a purchase loan to buy a house, while financing is certainly important, it's part of the process, not the entire process. You still buy the house, close the deal, furnish the new house, and so on.

The fact that refinancing has its own motivations suggests there should be an obvious reason for refinancing a mortgage loan. Refinances cost money and take time. I'm sure there are certainly other activities you'd rather be doing. That means that you shouldn't have to be "talked into" a refinance. Once you evaluate all your options, your costs, and your recovery period, the question of whether or not to refinance should be very clear to you. There are instances when a refinance is, in fact, not a "slam dunk," but could be in a gray area. You may face a longer recovery period or increasing interest rates, for example. But at the very least, a refinance does have its own set of rules that allows you to evaluate refinancing objectively.

Loan officers get paid when they close loans. If their pipeline is looking a little empty, they crack open their old "mortgage marketing" book and think up reasons why some of their past customers might benefit from a refinance. Some of those reasons are paying bills, college tuition, or shortening loan terms to save on interest. But by doing your homework and having the luxury of not being obligated to close within a particular time period, you should be able to find a loan officer who is truly dedicated to providing you with objective advice about a possible refinance loan. One way he can give objective advice is by providing guidance on interest-rate trends and loan programs that really meet your requirements—and not his sales quotas. Interest rates can move on a dime, but understanding how and why they move will always give you the upper hand. So does understanding closing costs and how to reduce or completely eliminate them in order to shorten your recovery period.

A refinance is a *choice*. It's a business decision. It should not be something you need to be talked into.

Glossary

Abstract of Title: A written record of the historical ownership of the property that helps to determine whether the property can, in fact, be transferred from one party to another without any previous claims. An abstract of title is used in certain parts of the country when determining if there are any previous claims on the subject property in question.

Acceleration: A loan accelerates when it is paid off early, usually at the request or demand of the lender. An acceleration clause within a loan document states what must happen when a loan must be paid immediately, but most usually it applies to nonpayment, late payments, or the transfer of the property without the lender's permission.

Adjustable Rate Mortgage (ARM): A loan program where the interest rate may change throughout the life of the loan. An ARM adjusts based on terms agreed to between the lender and the borrower, but typically it may only change once or twice a year.

Aggregator Site: A place where different lenders advertise their interest rates.

Alternate Credit: Items you must pay each month but that won't appear on your credit report. An alternate credit account might be your telephone bill. In relation to mortgage loans, while such items aren't reported as installment or revolving credit, they can establish your ability and willingness to make consistent payments in a responsible manner. Sometimes called *nonstandard credit*.

Alt Loans (Alternative loans): So-called because they're not conventional or government loans, but step outside the lending box and establish their own lending criteria.

Amortization: The length of time it takes for a loan to be fully paid off, by predetermined agreement. These payments are at regular intervals. Amortization terms can vary, but generally accepted terms run in 5-year increments, from 10 to 40 years. Sometimes called a *fully amortized loan.*

Annual Percentage Rate (APR): The cost of money borrowed, expressed as an annual rate. The APR is a useful consumer tool for comparing different lenders, but unfortunately it is often not used correctly. The APR can only work when comparing the same exact loan type from one lender to another.

Appraisable Asset: Any item whose value can be determined by a third-party expert. That car you want to sell is an appraisable asset. If the item can be appraised, then you can use those funds to buy a house.

Appraisal: A report that helps to determine the market value of a property. An appraisal can be done in various ways, as required by a lender, from simply driving by the property to ordering a full-blown inspection, complete with full-color photographs of the real estate. Appraisals compare similar homes in the area to substantiate the value of the property in question.

APR: See Annual Percentage Rate.

ARM: See Adjustable Rate Mortgage.

Assumable Mortgage: Homes sold with assumable mortgages let buyers take over the terms of the loan, along with the house being sold. Assumable loans may be fully or nonqualifying assumable, meaning buyers take over the loan without being qualified or otherwise evaluated by the original lender. Qualifying assumable loans mean that while buyers may assume terms of the existing note, they must qualify all over again, as if they were applying for a brand-new loan.

Automated Underwriting System (AUS): A software application that electronically issues a preliminary loan approval. An AUS uses a complex approval matrix that reviews credit reports, debt ratios, and other factors that go into a mortgage loan approval.

Automated Valuation Model (AVM): An electronic method of evaluating a property's appraised value, done by scanning public records for recent home sales and other data in the subject property's neighborhood. Although not yet widely accepted as a replacement for full-blown appraisals, many in the industry expect AVMs to eventually replace traditional appraisals altogether.

Balloon Mortgage: A type of mortgage where the remaining balance must be paid in full at the end of a preset term. A 5-year balloon mortgage might be amortized over a 30-year period, but the remaining balance is due, in full, at the end of 5 years.

Basis Point: Defined as 1/100 percent change in rate. A move of 50 basis points would cause a 30-year fixed-rate mortgage to change by 1/8 percent.

Bridge Loan: A short-term loan primarily used to pull equity out of one property for a down payment on another. This loan is paid off when the original property sells. Since they are short-term loans, sometimes lasting just a few weeks, usually only retail banks offer them. Usually, the borrower doesn't make any monthly payments and only pays off the loan when the property sells.

Bundling: The act of putting together several real estate or mortgage services in one package. Instead of paying for an appraisal here or an inspection there, some or all of the buyer's services are packaged together. Usually, a bundle offers discounts on all services, although when they're bundled, it's hard to parse all the services to see whether you're getting a good deal.

Buydown: Paying more money to get a lower interest rate is called a *permanent* buydown, and it is used in conjunction with discount points. The more points, the lower the rate. A *temporary* buydown is a fixed-rate mortgage that starts at a reduced rate for the first period, and then gradually increases to its final note rate. A temporary buydown for two years is called a 2–1 buydown. For three years, it's called a 3–2–1 buydown.

Cash-Out: A refinance mortgage that involves taking equity out of a home in the form of cash during a refinance. Instead of just reducing your interest rate during a refinance and financing your closing costs, you finance even more, putting the additional money in your pocket.

Churn: Refinancing over and over again, typically at the behest of a loan officer. Churning is usually associated with cashing out some equity, while at the same time paying off consumer debt or riding interest rates as they fall.

Closer: The person who helps prepare the lender's closing documents. The closer forwards those documents to your settlement agent's office, where you will be signing closing papers. In other states, a closer can be the person who holds your loan closing.

Closing Costs: The various fees involved when buying a home or obtaining a mortgage. The fees, required to issue a good loan, can come directly from the lender or may come from others in the transaction.

Collateral: Property owned by the borrower that's pledged to the lender as security in case the loan goes bad. A lender makes a mortgage, with the house as collateral.

Commodity: An item whose only determining value is price. For example, if a blue widget is the exact same at every widget store and is sold only at convenience stores, then the way to determine the best deal is not to look for differences between blue widgets—there are none—but by who has the lowest price.

Comparable Sales: Comparable sales are that part of an appraisal report that lists recent transfers of similar properties in the immediate vicinity of the house being bought. Also called *comps.*

Conforming Loan: A conventional Fannie Mae or Freddie Mac loan that is equal to or less than the maximum allowable loan limits established by Fannie and Freddie. These limits are changed annually.

Conventional Loan: A loan mortgage that uses guidelines established by Fannie Mae or Freddie Mac and is issued and guaranteed by lenders.

Correspondent Banker: A mortgage banker that doesn't intend to keep your mortgage loan but, instead, sells your loan to another preselected mortgage banker. Correspondent bankers are smaller mortgage bankers, those perhaps with a regional presence but not a national one. They can shop various rates from other correspondent mortgage bankers that have set up an established relationship to buy and sell loans from one another. Correspondent bankers operate much like a broker, except that they use their own money to fund loans.

Coupon: A Fannie Mae mortgage bond.

Credit Report: A report that shows the payment histories of a consumer, along with the individual's property, addresses, and any public records.

Credit Repository: A place where credit histories are stored. Merchants and banks agree to store consumers' credit patterns in a central place that other merchants and banks can access.

Credit Score: A number derived from a consumer's credit history and based upon various credit details in that consumer's past and upon the likelihood of default. Different credit patterns are assigned different numbers, and different credit activity may have a greater or lesser impact on the score. The higher the credit score, the better the credit.

Debt Consolidation: Paying off all or part of one's consumer debt with equity from a home. Debit consolidation can be part of a refinanced mortgage or a separate equity loan.

Debt Ratio: Gross monthly payments divided by gross monthly income, expressed as a percentage. There are typically two debt ratios to be considered: The *housing ratio*—sometimes called the *front-end* or *front ratio*—is the total monthly house payment, plus any monthly tax, insurance, private mortgage insurance, or homeowner's association dues, divided by gross monthly income. The *total debt ratio*—also called the *back-end* or *back ratio*—is the total housing payment, plus other monthly consumer installment or revolving debt, also expressed as a percentage. Loan debt ratio guidelines are usually denoted as 32/38, with 32 being the front ratio and the 38 being the back ratio. Ratio guidelines can vary from loan to loan and lender to lender.

Deed: A written document evidencing each transfer of ownership in a property.

Deed of Trust: A written document giving an interest in the home being bought to a third party, usually the lender, as security to the lender.

Delinquent: Being behind on a mortgage payment. Delinquencies typically begin to be recognized as 30 + days delinquent, 60 + days delinquent, and 90 + days delinquent.

Discount Points: Represented as a percentage of a loan amount. One point equals one percent of a loan balance. Borrowers pay discount points to reduce the interest rate for a mortgage. Typically, each discount point paid reduces the interest rate by $1/4$ percent. It's a form of prepaid interest to a lender. Also called *points*.

Document Stamp: Evidence—usually with an ink stamp—of how much tax was paid upon transfer of ownership of property. Certain states call it a doc stamp. Doc stamp tax rates can vary based upon locale, and not all states have doc stamps.

Down Payment: The amount of money initially given by the borrower to close a mortgage. The down payment equals the sales price less financing. It's the very first bit of equity you'll have in the new home.

Drive-By Appraisal: A type of appraisal in which the appraiser doesn't physically inspect the property, but conducts a visual inspection from the street.

Easement: A right of way previously established by a third party. Easement types can vary, but typically involve the right of a public utility to cross your land to access an electrical line.

Entitlement: The amount the VA will guarantee in order for a VA loan to be made. See also VA loan.

Equity: The difference between the appraised value of a home and any outstanding loans recorded against the house.

Escrow: Depending upon where you live, escrow can mean two things. On the West Coast, for example, when a home goes under contract, it "goes into escrow" (see also Escrow Agent). In other parts of the country, an escrow is a financial account set up by a lender to collect monthly installments for annual tax bills and/or hazard insurance policy renewals.

Escrow Account: See Impound Account.

Escrow Agent: On the West Coast, the escrow agent is the person or company that handles the home closing, ensuring that documents are assigned correctly and property transfer has legitimately changed hands.

FACTA: See Fair and Accurate Credit Transactions Act.

Fair and Accurate Credit Transactions Act (FACTA): New law that replaces the Fair Credit Reporting Act, or FCRA, and governs

how consumer information can be stored, shared, and moni-
tored for privacy and accuracy.

Fair Credit Reporting Act (FCRA): The first consumer law that em-
phasized consumer rights and protections relating to their
credit reports, their credit applications, and privacy concerns.

Fannie Mae: See Federal National Mortgage Association.

Farmers Home Administration (FmHA): Provides financing to
farmers and other qualified borrowers who are unable to obtain
loans elsewhere. These loans are typical for rural properties that
might be larger in acreage than a suburban home, as well as for
working farms.

FCRA: See Fair Credit Reporting Act.

Fed: Shorthand name for the Federal Reserve Board.

**Federal Home Loan Mortgage Corporation (FHLMC or Freddie
Mac):** A corporation established by the U.S. government in
1968 to buy mortgages from lenders who make loans under
Freddie Mac guidelines.

Federal Housing Administration (FHA): Formed in 1934 and now
a division of the Department of Housing and Urban Development (HUD). It provides loan guarantees to lenders who make
loans under FHA guidelines.

Federal National Mortgage Association (FNMA or Fannie Mae):
Originally established in 1938 by the U.S. government to buy
FHA mortgages and provide liquidity in the mortgage marketplace. It is similar in function to Freddie Mac. In 1968, its char-
ter was changed and it now purchases conventional mortgages,
as well as government ones.

Federal Reserve Board (The Fed): The head of the Federal Reserve
Banks, which, among other things, sets overnight lending rates
for banking institutions. The Fed does not set mortgage rates.

Fed Funds Rate: The rate that banks charge one another to borrow
money overnight.

Fee Income: The closing costs received by a lender or broker that is outside of the interest rate or discount points. Fee income can be in the form of loan processing charges, underwriting fees, and the like.

FHA: See Federal Housing Administration.

FICO: Stands for Fair Isaac Corporation, the company that invented the most widely used credit scoring system.

Final Inspection: The last inspection of a property, showing that a new home being built is 100 percent complete or that a home improvement is 100 percent complete. It lets lenders know that their collateral and their loan are exactly where they should be.

Financed Premium: An alternative to second mortgages and mortgage insurance that allows for the borrower to buy a mortgage insurance premium and roll the cost of the premium into the loan amount, in lieu of paying a mortgage insurance payment every month.

Fixed-Rate Mortgage: A loan whose interest rate does not change throughout the term of the loan.

Float: Actively deciding not to "lock" or guarantee an interest rate while a loan is being processed. A float is usually done because the borrower believes rates will go down.

Float-Down: A mortgage loan rate that can drop as mortgage rates drop. Usually, a loan comes in two types of float, one being during construction of a home and the other being during the period of an interest-rate lock.

Flood Certificate: A certificate that shows whether a property or part of a property lies above or below any local flood zones. These flood zones are mapped over the course of several years by the Federal Emergency Management Agency (FEMA). The certificate identifies the property's exact legal location and the flood line's elevation. There is a box that simply asks, "Is the property in a flood zone, yes or no?" If the property *is* in a flood zone, the lender will require special flood insurance that is not usually carried under a standard homeowner's hazard insurance policy.

FmHA: See Farmers Home Administration.

Foreclosure: The bad thing that happens when the mortgage isn't repaid. Lenders begin the process of forcefully recovering their collateral when borrowers fail to make loan payments. The lender takes your house away.

Freddie Mac: See Federal Home Loan Mortgage Corporation.

Fully Indexed Rate: The number reached when adding a loan's index and the margin. This rate is how adjustable note rates are compiled.

Funding: The actual transfer of money from a lender to a borrower.

Funding Fee: A required fee, equal to 2 percent of the sales price of a home, which helps to fund a VA loan guarantee.

Gift: When the down payment and closing costs for a home are given to the borrower, instead of the funds coming from their own accounts. Usually, such gifts can only come from family members or foundations established to help new homeowners.

Gift Affidavit: A signed form whereby someone swears that the money he's giving to you is indeed a gift, not a loan, and is to be used for the purchase of a home. Lenders like to see that form, as well as a paper trail of the gift funds being added to your own funds.

Gift Funds: Monies given to a borrower for the sole purpose of buying a home. These funds are not to be paid back in any form and are usually given by a family member or a qualified nonprofit organization.

Ginnie Mae: See Government National Mortgage Association.

Government National Mortgage Association (GNMA or Ginnie Mae): A U.S. government corporation formed to purchase government loans like VA and FHA loans from banks and mortgage lenders. Think of it as Fannie or Freddie, only it buys government loans.

Good Faith Estimate: A list of estimated closing costs on a particular mortgage transaction. This estimate must be provided to the loan applicants within 72 hours after receipt of a mortgage application by the lender or broker.

Hazard Insurance: A specific type of insurance that covers against certain destructive elements such as fire, wind, and hail. It is usually an addition to homeowner's insurance, but every home loan has a hazard rider.

HELOC: See Home Equity Line of Credit.

Hold-Back: A contingency fund associated with a construction or remodel. It covers any change orders that might occur during the process. A change order is what happens when you simply change your mind. The hold-back helps pay for the change, when changing your mind costs more than the loan. A typical hold-back amount is 10 percent of the original loan.

Home Equity Line of Credit (HELOC): A credit line using a home as collateral. Customers write checks on this line of credit whenever they need to and pay only on balances withdrawn. It is much like a credit card, but is secured by the property.

Homeowner's Insurance: An insurance policy that covers not just hazard items, but also other things, such as liability or personal property.

Housing GSEs (Government Sponsored Enterprises): Created to provide liquidity and stability in the home mortgage market, thereby increasing the flow of funds available to mortgage borrowers. Fannie Mae, Freddie Mac, and the Federal Home Loan Banks are, collectively, the housing GSEs.

Hybrid Loan: A cross between an ARM and a fixed-rate loan. In a hybrid loan, the rate is fixed for a predetermined number of years before turning into an adjustable rate mortgage, or ARM.

Impound Account: An account that is set up by a lender to deposit a monthly portion of annual property taxes or hazard insurance. As taxes or insurance come up for renewal, the lender pays the bill using these funds. Also called an *escrow account.*

Index: Used as the basis to establish an interest rate, usually associated with a margin. Most anything can be an index, but the most common are U.S. treasuries or similar instruments. See also Fully Indexed Rate.

Inspection: A structural review of the house to determine defects in workmanship, damage to the property, or required maintenance. A pest inspection, for example, looks for termites or wood ants. An inspection does not determine the value of the property.

Installment Account: Borrowing one lump sum and agreeing to pay back a certain amount each month until the loan is paid off. A car loan is an example of an installment loan.

Intangible Asset: An asset, not by itself, but by what it represents. A publicly traded stock is an intangible asset. It's not the stock itself that has the value, but what the stock represents in terms of income.

Intangible Tax: A state tax on personal property.

Interest-Only Loan: A loan that requires only that you pay the interest on your loan each month, without having to pay any part of the principal.

Interest Rate: The amount charged to borrow money over a specified period of time.

Interest Rate Reduction Loan (IRRL): A VA refinance loan program that has relaxed credit guidelines. Also called a *streamline refinance.*

IRRL: See Interest Rate Reduction Loan.

Jumbo Loan: A mortgage that exceeds current conforming loan limits. For 2007, anything above $417,000 is considered jumbo.

Junior Lien: A second mortgage or one that subordinates to another loan. Not as common a term as it used to be. You're more likely to hear references to a *second mortgage* or *piggyback*.

Junk Fees: Additional charges imposed by lenders, some of which are standard.

Land Contract: An arrangement where the buyer makes monthly payments to the seller, but the ownership of the property does not change hands until the loan is paid in full.

Land-to-Value: An appraisal term that calculates the value of the land as a percentage of the total value of the home. If the land exceeds the value of the home, it's more difficult to find financing without good comparable sales. Also called *lot-to-value*.

Lease-Purchase Agreement: An option whereby a buyer leases a home until he or she has saved up enough money for a down payment to qualify for a conventional mortgage. Also known as *rent-to-own*.

Lender Policy: Title insurance that protects a mortgage from defects or previous claims of ownership.

Liability: An obligation or bill on the part of the borrower. It works like an automobile loan. When you pay off the car, you get the title. Liabilities such as student loans or car payments can show up on a credit report, but they can also be anything else that you are obligated to pay. Those liabilities on the credit report are used to determine debt ratios.

LIBOR Index: See London Interbank Offered Rate.

Lien: A legal claim or prior interest on the property you're about to buy. Borrowing money from another source in order to buy a house could mean that someone else has a lien on that property.

Loan: Money granted to one party with the expectation of its being repaid.

Loan Officer: The person typically responsible for helping mortgage applicants get qualified and who also assists in loan selection and loan application. Loan officers can work at banks, credit unions, and mortgage brokerage houses, or for bankers.

Loan Processor: The person who gathers the required documentation for a loan application for loan submission. Along with your loan officer, you'll work with the loan processor quite a bit during your mortgage process.

Loan-to-Value Ratio (LTV): Expressed as a percentage of the loan amount when compared to the valuation of the home, determined by an appraisal. If a home were appraised at $100,000 and the loan amount was $70,000, then the LTV would be 70 percent.

Loan Underwriter: The person responsible for ultimately saying "yes" or "no" on a loan file. The underwriter compares loan guidelines with what you have documented in the file.

Lock: An agreement guaranteeing an interest rate over a predetermined period of time. Loan locks are not loan approvals; they're simply the rate your lender has agreed to give you at loan closing.

London Interbank Offered Rate (LIBOR): A British index similar to our Federal Funds rate, where British banks borrow money from one another over short periods in order to adhere to reserve requirements.

LTV: See Loan-to-Value Ratio.

Margin: A number, expressed as a percentage, which is added to a mortgage's index to determine the rate the borrower pays on the note. An index can be a six-month CD at 4 percent, and the margin can be 2 percent. The interest rate the borrower pays is 4 + 2, or 6 percent. A fully indexed rate is the index plus the margin.

Market Gain: The difference between what a mortgage price was when you locked it with the lender and what the mortgage price is when the loan is physically locked with the lender's secondary department or with a mortgage broker's wholesale lender.

Market Value: In an open market, both the highest the borrower is willing to pay and the least the seller is willing to accept at the time of contract. Property appraisals help justify market value by comparing similar home sales in the subject property's neighborhood.

Modifiable Mortgage: A mortgage loan that allows its interest rate to be modified, even if it's at another lender.

Mortgage: A loan, with the property being pledged as collateral. The mortgage is retired when the loan is paid in full.

Mortgage-Backed Securities: Investment securities issued by Wall Street firms that are guaranteed, or collateralized, with home mortgages taken out by consumers. These securities can then be bought and sold on Wall Street.

Mortgage Bankers: Lenders who use their own funds to lend money. Historically, these funds would have come from the savings accounts of other bank customers, but with the evolution of mortgage banking, that's the old way of doing business. Even though bankers use their own money, it may come from other sources, such as lines of credit or through selling loans to other institutions.

Mortgage Brokers: Companies that set up a home loan between a banker and a borrower. Brokers don't have money to lend directly, but they have experience in finding various loan programs that can suit the borrower, similar to how an independent insurance agent operates. Brokers don't work for the borrower but, instead, provide mortgage loan choices from other mortgage lenders.

Mortgagee: The person or business making the loan. Also called the *lender*.

Mortgage Insurance (MI): See Private Mortgage Insurance.

Mortgagor: The person(s) getting the loan. Also called the *borrower*.

Multiple Listing Service (MLS): A central repository where real estate brokers and agents show homes and search for homes that are for sale.

Negative Amortization (neg-am loan): An adjustable rate mortgage that can have two interest rates—the contract rate or the fully indexed rate. The contract rate is the minimum agreed-upon rate the consumer may pay; sometimes the contract rate is lower than the fully indexed rate. The borrower has a choice of which rate to pay, but if the contract rate is lower than the fully indexed rate, that difference is added back to the loan. If your contract payments are only $500, but the fully indexed rate is $700 and you pay only the contract rate, $200 is added back into your original loan amount. These loans are not for the fainthearted or for those with little money down.

NINA (No Income, No Asset mortgage): A type of loan that does not require that the borrower prove or otherwise document any income or asset whatsoever.

No-Fee Loan: A loan where your lender pays closing costs for you, if you agree to a slightly higher interest rate.

Nonconforming: Loans whose amounts are above current Fannie or Freddie limits. See also Jumbo Loan.

Note: A promise to repay. It may or may not have property involved, and it may or may not be a mortgage.

Note Modification: Taking the original terms of a note and, without changing any other part of the obligation or title, reducing the interest rate for the remaining term of the loan. A note modification means you can't "shop around" in order to reduce your rate; instead, you must work with your original lender who still services your mortgage. In a modification, nothing can change except the rate.

One-Time Close Loan: A construction loan whereby you obtain con-

struction financing, permanent financing, and lock in a permanent mortgage rate at the same time. See also Two-Time Close
Loan.

Origination Fee: A fee charged to cover costs associated with finding, documenting, and preparing a mortgage application. It's
usually expressed as a percentage of the loan amount.

Owner's Policy: Title insurance made for the benefit of the homeowner.

Par: An interest rate that can be obtained without paying any discount points and that does not have any additional yield beyond
its rate. For instance, you get a 30-year quote of 7 percent with
1 point, or 7.25 percent with zero points, or 7.50 percent with
zero points, plus an additional yield to you of $1,000 toward
closing costs. Here, the 7.25 percent at zero points is the par
rate.

Payment Option ARM: A type of negative amortization loan where
you have a choice as to what you'd like to pay each month. The
choice is between an initial contract rate, an interest-only, or a
fully indexed, fully amortized loan.

Payment Shock: A term used by lenders referring to the percentage
difference between what you're paying now for housing and
what your new payment would be. Most loan programs don't
have a payment shock provision, but for those that do, a common percentage increase is 150 percent.

Permanent Buydown: See Buydown.

Piggyback Mortgage: See Second Mortgage.

PITI (Principal, Interest, Taxes, and Insurance): These figures are
used to help determine front debt ratios.

Pledged Asset: An appraisable property or security that is collateralized to make a mortgage loan. Sometimes, a pledged asset can
be a stock or mutual fund. A lender can make a mortgage loan
and use the mutual fund as part of the collateral. If the borrower

fails to make the payments, all or part of the pledged asset can go to the lender.

PMI: See Private Mortgage Insurance.

Points: See Discount Points.

Portfolio Loan: A loan made by a direct lender, usually a bank, and kept in the lender's loan portfolio instead of being sold or underwritten to any external guidelines.

Predatory Loan: A loan designed to take advantage of people by charging either too many fees, too high an interest rate, or both, while also stripping the homeowners of their equity.

Prepaid Interest: Daily interest collected from the day of a loan closing to the first of the following month.

Prepayment Penalty: An amount paid to the lender if the loan is paid off before its maturity, or if extra payments are made on the loan. A hard penalty is automatic if the loan is paid off early or if extra payments are made at any time, for any amount whatsoever. A soft penalty only lasts for a couple of years and may allow extra payments on the loan, not to exceed a certain amount.

Principal: The outstanding amount owed on a loan, not including any interest due.

Private Mortgage Insurance (PMI): Typically required on all mortgage loans with less than 20 percent down. It is an insurance policy, paid by the borrower, with benefits paid to the lender. It covers the difference between the borrower's down payment and 20 percent of the sales price. If the borrower defaults on the mortgage, this difference is paid to the lender.

Pull-Through Rate: A term, used by wholesale lenders, to track the percentage of loans that close and that have been locked by a broker.

Quit Claim: A release of any interest in a property from one party to another. A quit claim does not, however, release the obligation on the mortgage.

Rate-and-Term Refinance: Refinancing to get a new rate. You're changing the interest rate and changing the term, or length, of the new note.

Rate Cap: How high your ARM rate is permitted to change at each adjustment period. There are three possible caps on an adjustable rate mortgage: the *adjustment cap,* the *lifetime rate cap,* and the *initial rate cap.*

Real Estate Account: A mortgage secured by real estate.

Realtor: A member of the National Association of Realtors, and a registered trademark. Not all real estate agents are Realtors.

Recast: A term applied to ARMs and used when extra payments are made to the principal balance. When a note is recast, your monthly payment is calculated for you.

Recurring Closing Costs: Items such as interest charges, insurance, and property taxes that occur again and again as part of the closing costs.

Refinance: Obtaining a new mortgage to replace an existing one. There is also a *rate-and-term refinance,* where only the outstanding principal balance, interest due, and closing costs are included in the loan.

Reissue: When refinancing, there may be discounts if you use the same title agency. This "reissue" of an original title report can cost much less than a full title insurance policy.

Release of Lien: See Warranty Deed.

Rescission: Withdrawal from a mortgage agreement. Refinanced mortgage loans for a primary residence have a required three-day "cooling off" period before the loan becomes official. If, for any reason, you decide not to take the mortgage, you can rescind, and the whole deal's off.

Reserves: A borrower's assets after closing. Reserves can include cash in the bank, stocks, mutual funds, retirement accounts, IRAs, and 401(k) accounts.

Reverse Mortgage: A mortgage designed to help older Americans who own their homes by paying homeowners cash, in exchange for the equity in their homes. When a homeowner no longer owns the home (by selling, moving out, or dying), then the reverse mortgage lender is paid back all the money borrowed, plus interest.

Revolving Account: A credit card or department store account on which you typically have a limit and don't make any payments until you charge something.

Sales Contract: Your written agreement to sell or purchase a home, signed by both the seller and buyer.

Secondary Market: A financial arena where mortgages are bought and sold, either individually or grouped together into securities backed by those mortgages. Fannie Mae and Freddie Mac are the backbone for the conventional secondary market. Other secondary markets exist for nonconforming loans, subprime loans, and others.

Second Mortgage: Sometimes called a *piggyback* mortgage, a second mortgage assumes a subordinate position behind a first mortgage. If a home goes into foreclosure, the first mortgage would be settled before the second could lay claim. See also Junior Lien.

Seller: The person transferring ownership and all rights for your home, in exchange for cash or trade.

Settlement Statement: Shows all financial entries during the home sale, including sales price, closing costs, loan amounts, and property taxes. Your initial good faith estimate will be your first glimpse of your settlement statement. This statement is one of the final documents put together before you go to closing, and is prepared by your attorney or settlement agent. Also called the Final HUD-1.

Subprime Loan: A loan made to people with less than "prime" credit. There are various stages of subprime credit, from loans for those with simply "tarnished" credit who can't quite get a conventional mortgage, to those with seriously damaged credit who may be in or just out of bankruptcy, or who might have collection accounts or judgments and liens against them.

Survey: A map that shows the physical location of the structure and where it sits on the property. A survey also designates any easements that run across or through the property.

Tangible Net Benefit: A benefit analysis administered by state governments to help determine whether or not a refinance is right for you.

Temporary Buydown: See Buydown.

Throwaway Fee: A fee that loan officers use in the negotiation process. The other type of fee is a *required* one.

Title: Legal ownership in a property.

Title Exam/Title Search: The process where public records are reviewed in order to research any previous liens on the property.

Title Insurance: Protection for the lender, the seller, and/or the borrower against any defects or previous claims to the property being transferred or sold.

Two-Time Close Loan: A method of construction financing, whereby you first get a construction loan and then get another mortgage at the end of construction. You'll go to two different closings for a two-time close loan. See also One-Time Close Loan.

VA Loan: Government mortgage guaranteed by the Department of Veterans Affairs.

VA No-No: A type of VA loan where the borrower not only puts no money down, but also pays no closing costs.

Verification of Deposit (VOD): A form mailed to a bank or credit union that asks the institution to verify that a borrower's bank account exists, how much is in it, how long the borrower has had it, and what the average balance was over the previous two months.

VOD: See Verification of Deposit.

Warranty Deed: A document that each lien holder must sign, absolving him of any future interest. Also known as *release of lien*.

Wraparound Mortgage: A method of financing where the borrower pays the former owner of the property each month, in the form of a mortgage payment. The former owner will then make a mortgage payment to the original mortgage holder.

Yield Spread Premium (YSP): A fee paid by the lender to the broker, in exchange for a higher interest rate or for an above-wholesale rate. Though the borrower may qualify for a certain rate, the broker may charge this fee in order to make a bigger commission, which gives the borrower a slightly higher rate. This practice was originally intended as a way to avoid charging the borrower any out-of-pocket fees. However, many feel the intentions have been misguided, and that it's ended up as just another fee the borrower gets stuck with.

Appendix:

Monthly Payment Schedules

The following schedule shows monthly payments per thousand dollars financed. To calculate your monthly payment:

1. Find your interest rate in the first column.

2. Move across to the appropriate column for your term.

3. Multiply that number by the number of thousand dollars financed.

Example

If you are borrowing $150,000 at 6.50 percent interest for a 30-year term:

> $6.32 × 150 (thousands) = $948.00 principal and interest payment

Thus, your monthly payment for both principal and interest is $948.

Rate	40 years	30 years	25 years	20 years	15 years	10 years
2.500	$3.30	$3.95	$4.49	$5.30	$6.67	$9.43
2.625	$3.37	$4.02	$4.55	$5.36	$6.73	$9.48
2.750	$3.44	$4.08	$4.61	$5.42	$6.79	$9.54
2.875	$3.51	$4.15	$4.68	$5.48	$6.85	$9.60
3.000	$3.58	$4.22	$4.74	$5.55	$6.91	$9.66
3.125	$3.65	$4.28	$4.81	$5.61	$6.97	$9.71
3.250	$3.73	$4.35	$4.87	$5.67	$7.03	$9.77
3.375	$3.80	$4.42	$4.94	$5.74	$7.09	$9.83
3.500	$3.87	$4.49	$5.01	$5.80	$7.15	$9.89
3.625	$3.95	$4.56	$5.07	$5.86	$7.21	$9.95
3.750	$4.03	$4.63	$5.14	$5.93	$7.27	$10.01
3.875	$4.10	$4.70	$5.21	$5.99	$7.33	$10.07
4.000	$4.18	$4.77	$5.28	$6.06	$7.40	$10.12
4.125	$4.26	$4.85	$5.35	$6.13	$7.46	$10.18
4.250	$4.34	$4.92	$5.42	$6.19	$7.52	$10.24
4.375	$4.42	$4.99	$5.49	$6.26	$7.59	$10.30
4.500	$4.50	$5.07	$5.56	$6.33	$7.65	$10.36
4.625	$4.58	$5.14	$5.63	$6.39	$7.71	$10.42
4.750	$4.66	$5.22	$5.70	$6.46	$7.78	$10.48
4.875	$4.74	$5.29	$5.77	$6.53	$7.84	$10.55
5.000	$4.82	$5.37	$5.85	$6.60	$7.91	$10.61
5.125	$4.91	$5.44	$5.92	$6.67	$7.97	$10.67
5.250	$4.99	$5.52	$5.99	$6.74	$8.04	$10.73
5.375	$5.07	$5.60	$6.07	$6.81	$8.10	$10.79
5.500	$5.16	$5.68	$6.14	$6.88	$8.17	$10.85
5.625	$5.24	$5.76	$6.22	$6.95	$8.24	$10.91
5.750	$5.33	$5.84	$6.29	$7.02	$8.30	$10.98
5.875	$5.42	$5.92	$6.37	$7.09	$8.37	$11.04
6.000	$5.50	$6.00	$6.44	$7.16	$8.44	$11.10
6.125	$5.59	$6.08	$6.52	$7.24	$8.51	$11.16
6.250	$5.68	$6.16	$6.60	$7.31	$8.57	$11.23
6.375	$5.77	$6.24	$6.67	$7.38	$8.64	$11.29

Rate	40 years	30 years	25 years	20 years	15 years	10 years
6.500	$5.85	$6.32	$6.75	$7.46	$8.71	$11.35
6.625	$5.94	$6.40	$6.83	$7.53	$8.78	$11.42
6.750	$6.03	$6.49	$6.91	$7.60	$8.85	$11.48
6.875	$6.12	$6.57	$6.99	$7.68	$8.92	$11.55
7.000	$6.21	$6.65	$7.07	$7.75	$8.99	$11.61
7.125	$6.31	$6.74	$7.15	$7.83	$9.06	$11.68
7.250	$6.40	$6.82	$7.23	$7.90	$9.13	$11.74
7.375	$6.49	$6.91	$7.31	$7.98	$9.20	$11.81
7.500	$6.58	$6.99	$7.39	$8.06	$9.27	$11.87
7.625	$6.67	$7.08	$7.47	$8.13	$9.34	$11.94
7.750	$6.77	$7.16	$7.55	$8.21	$9.41	$12.00
7.875	$6.86	$7.25	$7.64	$8.29	$9.48	$12.07
8.000	$6.95	$7.34	$7.72	$8.36	$9.56	$12.13
8.125	$7.05	$7.42	$7.80	$8.44	$9.63	$12.20
8.250	$7.14	$7.51	$7.88	$8.52	$9.70	$12.27
8.375	$7.24	$7.60	$7.97	$8.60	$9.77	$12.33
8.500	$7.33	$7.69	$8.05	$8.68	$9.85	$12.40
8.625	$7.43	$7.78	$8.14	$8.76	$9.92	$12.47
8.750	$7.52	$7.87	$8.22	$8.84	$9.99	$12.53
8.875	$7.62	$7.96	$8.31	$8.92	$10.07	$12.60
9.000	$7.71	$8.05	$8.39	$9.00	$10.14	$12.67
9.125	$7.81	$8.14	$8.48	$9.08	$10.22	$12.74
9.250	$7.91	$8.23	$8.56	$9.16	$10.29	$12.80
9.375	$8.00	$8.32	$8.65	$9.24	$10.37	$12.87
9.500	$8.10	$8.41	$8.74	$9.32	$10.44	$12.94
9.625	$8.20	$8.50	$8.82	$9.40	$10.52	$13.01
9.750	$8.30	$8.59	$8.91	$9.49	$10.59	$13.08
9.875	$8.39	$8.68	$9.00	$9.57	$10.67	$13.15
10.000	$8.49	$8.78	$9.09	$9.65	$10.75	$13.22
10.125	$8.59	$8.87	$9.18	$9.73	$10.82	$13.28
10.250	$8.69	$8.96	$9.26	$9.82	$10.90	$13.35
10.375	$8.79	$9.05	$9.35	$9.90	$10.98	$13.42

Rate	40 years	30 years	25 years	20 years	15 years	10 years
10.500	$8.89	$9.15	$9.44	$9.98	$11.05	$13.49
10.625	$8.98	$9.24	$9.53	$10.07	$11.13	$13.56
10.750	$9.08	$9.33	$9.62	$10.15	$11.21	$13.63
10.875	$9.18	$9.43	$9.71	$10.24	$11.29	$13.70
11.000	$9.28	$9.52	$9.80	$10.32	$11.37	$13.78
11.125	$9.38	$9.62	$9.89	$10.41	$11.44	$13.85
11.250	$9.48	$9.71	$9.98	$10.49	$11.52	$13.92
11.375	$9.58	$9.81	$10.07	$10.58	$11.60	$13.99
11.500	$9.68	$9.90	$10.16	$10.66	$11.68	$14.06
11.625	$9.78	$10.00	$10.26	$10.75	$11.76	$14.13
11.750	$9.88	$10.09	$10.35	$10.84	$11.84	$14.20
11.875	$9.98	$10.19	$10.44	$10.92	$11.92	$14.27
12.000	$10.08	$10.29	$10.53	$11.01	$12.00	$14.35
12.125	$10.19	$10.38	$10.62	$11.10	$12.08	$14.42
12.250	$10.29	$10.48	$10.72	$11.19	$12.16	$14.49
12.375	$10.39	$10.58	$10.81	$11.27	$12.24	$14.56
12.500	$10.49	$10.67	$10.90	$11.36	$12.33	$14.64
12.625	$10.59	$10.77	$11.00	$11.45	$12.41	$14.71
12.750	$10.69	$10.87	$11.09	$11.54	$12.49	$14.78
12.875	$10.79	$10.96	$11.18	$11.63	$12.57	$14.86
13.000	$10.90	$11.06	$11.28	$11.72	$12.65	$14.93
13.125	$11.00	$11.16	$11.37	$11.80	$12.73	$15.00
13.250	$11.10	$11.26	$11.47	$11.89	$12.82	$15.08
13.375	$11.20	$11.36	$11.56	$11.98	$12.90	$15.15
13.500	$11.30	$11.45	$11.66	$12.07	$12.98	$15.23
13.625	$11.40	$11.55	$11.75	$12.16	$13.07	$15.30
13.750	$11.51	$11.65	$11.85	$12.25	$13.15	$15.38
13.875	$11.61	$11.75	$11.94	$12.34	$13.23	$15.45
14.000	$11.71	$11.85	$12.04	$12.44	$13.32	$15.53
14.125	$11.81	$11.95	$12.13	$12.53	$13.40	$15.60
14.250	$11.92	$12.05	$12.23	$12.62	$13.49	$15.68
14.375	$12.02	$12.15	$12.33	$12.71	$13.57	$15.75

Rate	40 years	30 years	25 years	20 years	15 years	10 years
14.500	$12.12	$12.25	$12.42	$12.80	$13.66	$15.83
14.625	$12.22	$12.35	$12.52	$12.89	$13.74	$15.90
14.750	$12.33	$12.44	$12.61	$12.98	$13.83	$15.98
14.875	$12.43	$12.54	$12.71	$13.08	$13.91	$16.06
15.000	$12.53	$12.64	$12.81	$13.17	$14.00	$16.13
15.125	$12.64	$12.74	$12.91	$13.26	$14.08	$16.21
15.250	$12.74	$12.84	$13.00	$13.35	$14.17	$16.29
15.375	$12.84	$12.94	$13.10	$13.45	$14.25	$16.36
15.500	$12.94	$13.05	$13.20	$13.54	$14.34	$16.44
15.625	$13.05	$13.15	$13.30	$13.63	$14.43	$16.52
15.750	$13.15	$13.25	$13.39	$13.73	$14.51	$16.60
15.875	$13.25	$13.35	$13.49	$13.82	$14.60	$16.67
16.000	$13.36	$13.45	$13.59	$13.91	$14.69	$16.75
16.125	$13.46	$13.55	$13.69	$14.01	$14.77	$16.83
16.250	$13.56	$13.65	$13.79	$14.10	$14.86	$16.91
16.375	$13.67	$13.75	$13.88	$14.19	$14.95	$16.99
16.500	$13.77	$13.85	$13.98	$14.29	$15.04	$17.06
16.625	$13.87	$13.95	$14.08	$14.38	$15.13	$17.14
16.750	$13.98	$14.05	$14.18	$14.48	$15.21	$17.22
16.875	$14.08	$14.16	$14.28	$14.57	$15.30	$17.30
17.000	$14.18	$14.26	$14.38	$14.67	$15.39	$17.38
17.125	$14.29	$14.36	$14.48	$14.76	$15.48	$17.46
17.250	$14.39	$14.46	$14.58	$14.86	$15.57	$17.54
17.375	$14.49	$14.56	$14.68	$14.95	$15.66	$17.62
17.500	$14.60	$14.66	$14.78	$15.05	$15.75	$17.70
17.625	$14.70	$14.77	$14.87	$15.15	$15.84	$17.78
17.750	$14.80	$14.87	$14.97	$15.24	$15.92	$17.86
17.875	$14.91	$14.97	$15.07	$15.34	$16.01	$17.94
18.000	$15.01	$15.07	$15.17	$15.43	$16.10	$18.02

Index